HBR'S 10 MUST READS

On
AI, Analytics, and the New Machine Age

HBR's 10 Must Reads series is the definitive collection of ideas
and best practices for aspiring and experienced leaders alike.
These books offer essential reading selected from the pages
of *Harvard Business Review* on topics critical to the success of
every manager.

Titles include:

HBR's 10 Must Reads 2015
HBR's 10 Must Reads 2016
HBR's 10 Must Reads 2017
HBR's 10 Must Reads 2018
HBR's 10 Must Reads 2019
HBR's 10 Must Reads for New Managers
HBR's 10 Must Reads on AI, Analytics, and the New Machine Age
HBR's 10 Must Reads on Change Management
HBR's 10 Must Reads on Collaboration
HBR's 10 Must Reads on Communication
HBR's 10 Must Reads on Emotional Intelligence
HBR's 10 Must Reads on Entrepreneurship and Startups
HBR's 10 Must Reads on Innovation
HBR's 10 Must Reads on Leadership
HBR's 10 Must Reads on Leadership for Healthcare
HBR's 10 Must Reads on Leadership Lessons from Sports
HBR's 10 Must Reads on Making Smart Decisions
HBR's 10 Must Reads on Managing Across Cultures
HBR's 10 Must Reads on Managing People
HBR's 10 Must Reads on Managing Yourself
HBR's 10 Must Reads on Mental Toughness
HBR's 10 Must Reads on Sales
HBR's 10 Must Reads on Strategic Marketing
HBR's 10 Must Reads on Strategy
HBR's 10 Must Reads on Strategy for Healthcare
HBR's 10 Must Reads on Teams
HBR's 10 Must Reads on Women and Leadership
HBR's 10 Must Reads: The Essentials

HBR'S 10 MUST READS

On
AI, Analytics, and the New Machine Age

HARVARD BUSINESS REVIEW PRESS
Boston, Massachusetts

Library of Congress Cataloging-in-Publication data

Title: HBR's 10 must reads on AI, analytics, and the new machine age.
Other titles: Harvard Business Review's ten must reads on AI, analytics, and the new machine age | On AI, analytics, and the new machine age. | AI, analytics, and the new machine age. | Artificial intelligence, analytics, and the new machine age. | Harvard business review. | HBR's 10 must reads (Series)
Description: Boston, Massachusetts : Harvard Business Review Press, [2018] | Series: HBR's 10 must reads series | Articles previously published in Harvard Business Review.
Identifiers: LCCN 2018029344 | ISBN 978-1-63369-686-0
Subjects: LCSH: Artificial intelligence. | Disruptive technologies. | Data mining. | Industrial management.
Classification: LCC TA347.A78 H456 2018 | DDC 658.4/038—dc23
LC record available at https://lccn.loc.gov/2018029344

Contents

On
AI, Analytics,
and the New
Machine Age

Artificial Intelligence for the Real World

by Thomas H. Davenport and Rajeev Ronanki

IN 2013, THE MD ANDERSON CANCER CENTER launched a "moon shot" project: diagnose and recommend treatment plans for certain forms of cancer using IBM's Watson cognitive system. But in 2017, the project was put on hold after costs topped $62 million—and the system had yet to be used on patients. At the same time, the cancer center's IT group was experimenting with using cognitive technologies to do much less ambitious jobs, such as making hotel and restaurant recommendations for patients' families, determining which patients needed help paying bills, and addressing staff IT problems. The results of these projects have been much more promising: The new systems have contributed to increased patient satisfaction, improved financial performance, and a decline in time spent on tedious data entry by the hospital's care managers. Despite the setback on the moon shot, MD Anderson remains committed to using cognitive technology—that is, next-generation artificial intelligence—to enhance cancer treatment, and is currently developing a variety of new projects at its center of competency for cognitive computing.

The contrast between the two approaches is relevant to anyone planning AI initiatives. Our survey of 250 executives who are familiar with their companies' use of cognitive technology shows that three-quarters of them believe that AI will substantially transform their companies within three years. However, our study of

152 projects in almost as many companies also reveals that highly ambitious moon shots are less likely to be successful than "low-hanging fruit" projects that enhance business processes. This shouldn't be surprising—such has been the case with the great majority of new technologies that companies have adopted in the past. But the hype surrounding artificial intelligence has been especially powerful, and some organizations have been seduced by it.

In this article, we'll look at the various categories of AI being employed and provide a framework for how companies should begin to build up their cognitive capabilities in the next several years to achieve their business objectives.

Three Types of AI

It is useful for companies to look at AI through the lens of business capabilities rather than technologies. Broadly speaking, AI can support three important business needs: automating business processes, gaining insight through data analysis, and engaging with customers and employees. (See the exhibit "Cognitive projects by type.")

Process automation

Of the 152 projects we studied, the most common type was the automation of digital and physical tasks—typically back-office administrative and financial activities—using robotic process automation

Cognitive projects by type

We studied 152 cognitive technology projects and found that they fell into three categories.

Robotics & cognitive automation:	Cognitive insight:	Cognitive engagement:
71	57	24

Idea in Brief

The Problem

Cognitive technologies are increasingly being used to solve business problems, but many of the most ambitious AI projects encounter setbacks or fail.

The Approach

Companies should take an incremental rather than a transformative approach and focus on augmenting rather than replacing human capabilities.

The Process

To get the most out of AI, firms must understand which technologies perform what types of tasks, create a prioritized portfolio of projects based on business needs, and develop plans to scale up across the company.

technologies. RPA is more advanced than earlier business-process automation tools, because the "robots" (that is, code on a server) act like a human inputting and consuming information from multiple IT systems. Tasks include:

- transferring data from e-mail and call center systems into systems of record—for example, updating customer files with address changes or service additions;

- replacing lost credit or ATM cards, reaching into multiple systems to update records and handle customer communications;

- reconciling failures to charge for services across billing systems by extracting information from multiple document types; and

- "reading" legal and contractual documents to extract provisions using natural language processing.

RPA is the least expensive and easiest to implement of the cognitive technologies we'll discuss here, and typically brings a quick and high return on investment. (It's also the least "smart" in the sense that these applications aren't programmed to learn and improve,

The business benefits of AI

We surveyed 250 executives who were familiar with their companies' use of cognitive technologies to learn about their goals for AI initiatives. More than half said their primary goal was to make existing products better. Reducing head count was mentioned by only 22%.

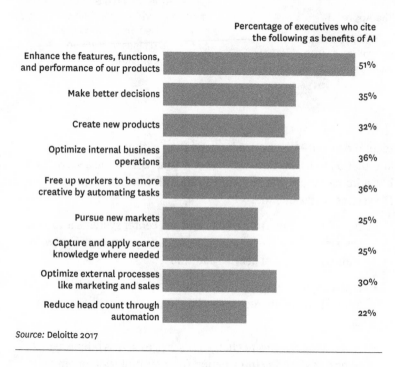

Percentage of executives who cite
the following as benefits of AI

Enhance the features, functions, and performance of our products	51%
Make better decisions	35%
Create new products	32%
Optimize internal business operations	36%
Free up workers to be more creative by automating tasks	36%
Pursue new markets	25%
Capture and apply scarce knowledge where needed	25%
Optimize external processes like marketing and sales	30%
Reduce head count through automation	22%

Source: Deloitte 2017

though developers are slowly adding more intelligence and learning capability.) It is particularly well suited to working across multiple back-end systems.

At NASA, cost pressures led the agency to launch four RPA pilots in accounts payable and receivable, IT spending, and human resources—all managed by a shared services center. The four projects worked well—in the HR application, for example, 86% of transactions were completed without human intervention—and are being

The challenges of AI

Executives in our survey identified several factors that can stall or derail AI initiatives, ranging from integration issues to scarcity of talent.

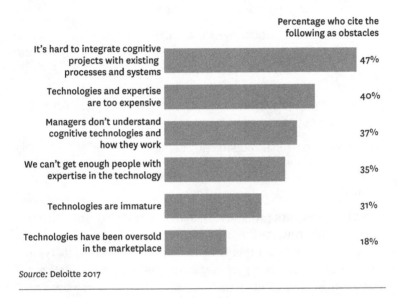

Percentage who cite the following as obstacles

It's hard to integrate cognitive projects with existing processes and systems	47%
Technologies and expertise are too expensive	40%
Managers don't understand cognitive technologies and how they work	37%
We can't get enough people with expertise in the technology	35%
Technologies are immature	31%
Technologies have been oversold in the marketplace	18%

Source: Deloitte 2017

rolled out across the organization. NASA is now implementing more RPA bots, some with higher levels of intelligence. As Jim Walker, project leader for the shared services organization notes, "So far it's not rocket science."

One might imagine that robotic process automation would quickly put people out of work. But across the 71 RPA projects we reviewed (47% of the total), replacing administrative employees was neither the primary objective nor a common outcome. Only a few projects led to reductions in head count, and in most cases, the tasks in question had already been shifted to outsourced workers. As technology improves, robotic automation projects are likely to lead to some job losses in the future, particularly in the offshore business-process outsourcing industry. If you can outsource a task, you can probably automate it.

Cognitive insight

The second most common type of project in our study (38% of the total) used algorithms to detect patterns in vast volumes of data and interpret their meaning. Think of it as "analytics on steroids." These machine-learning applications are being used to:

- predict what a particular customer is likely to buy;

- identify credit fraud in real time and detect insurance claims fraud;

- analyze warranty data to identify safety or quality problems in automobiles and other manufactured products;

- automate personalized targeting of digital ads; and

- provide insurers with more-accurate and detailed actuarial modeling.

Cognitive insights provided by machine learning differ from those available from traditional analytics in three ways: They are usually much more data-intensive and detailed, the models typically are trained on some part of the data set, and the models get better—that is, their ability to use new data to make predictions or put things into categories improves over time.

Versions of machine learning (deep learning, in particular, which attempts to mimic the activity in the human brain in order to recognize patterns) can perform feats such as recognizing images and speech. Machine learning can also make available new data for better analytics. While the activity of data curation has historically been quite labor-intensive, now machine learning can identify probabilistic matches—data that is likely to be associated with the same person or company but that appears in slightly different formats—across databases. GE has used this technology to integrate supplier data and has saved $80 million in its first year by eliminating redundancies and negotiating contracts that were previously managed at the business unit level. Similarly, a large bank used this technology to extract data on terms from supplier contracts and match it with invoice numbers, identifying tens of millions of dollars in products and services not supplied. Deloitte's audit practice is using cognitive insight to extract terms from contracts, which enables an audit to address a much higher proportion of documents, often 100%, without human auditors' having to painstakingly read through them.

Cognitive insight applications are typically used to improve performance on jobs only machines can do—tasks such as programmatic ad buying that involve such high-speed data crunching and automation that they've long been beyond human ability—so they're not generally a threat to human jobs.

Cognitive engagement

Projects that engage employees and customers using natural language processing chatbots, intelligent agents, and machine learning were the least common type in our study (accounting for 16% of the total). This category includes:

- intelligent agents that offer 24/7 customer service addressing a broad and growing array of issues from password requests to technical support questions—all in the customer's natural language;

- internal sites for answering employee questions on topics including IT, employee benefits, and HR policy;

- product and service recommendation systems for retailers that increase personalization, engagement, and sales—typically including rich language or images; and

- health treatment recommendation systems that help providers create customized care plans that take into account individual patients' health status and previous treatments.

The companies in our study tended to use cognitive engagement technologies more to interact with employees than with customers. That may change as firms become more comfortable turning customer interactions over to machines. Vanguard, for example, is piloting an intelligent agent that helps its customer service staff answer frequently asked questions. The plan is to eventually allow customers to engage with the cognitive agent directly, rather than with the human customer-service agents. SEBank, in Sweden, and the medical technology giant Becton, Dickinson, in the United States, are using the lifelike intelligent-agent avatar Amelia to serve as an internal employee help desk for IT support. SEBank has recently made Amelia available to customers on a limited basis in order to test its performance and customer response.

Companies tend to take a conservative approach to customer-facing cognitive engagement technologies largely because of their immaturity. Facebook, for example, found that its Messenger chatbots couldn't answer 70% of customer requests without human intervention. As a result, Facebook and several other firms are restricting bot-based interfaces to certain topic domains or conversation types.

Our research suggests that cognitive engagement apps are not currently threatening customer service or sales rep jobs. In most of the projects we studied, the goal was not to reduce head count but to handle growing numbers of employee and customer interactions without adding staff. Some organizations were planning to hand over routine communications to machines, while transitioning customer-support personnel to more-complex activities such as handling customer issues that escalate, conducting extended unstructured dialogues, or reaching out to customers before they call in with problems.

As companies become more familiar with cognitive tools, they are experimenting with projects that combine elements from all three categories to reap the benefits of AI. An Italian insurer, for example, developed a "cognitive help desk" within its IT organization. The system engages with employees using deep-learning technology (part of the cognitive insights category) to search frequently asked questions and answers, previously resolved cases, and documentation to come up with solutions to employees' problems. It uses a smart-routing capability (business process automation) to forward the most complex problems to human representatives, and it uses natural language processing to support user requests in Italian.

Despite their rapidly expanding experience with cognitive tools, however, companies face significant obstacles in development and implementation. On the basis of our research, we've developed a four-step framework for integrating AI technologies that can help companies achieve their objectives, whether the projects are moon shoots or business-process enhancements.

1. Understanding the Technologies

Before embarking on an AI initiative, companies must understand which technologies perform what types of tasks, and the strengths and limitations of each. Rule-based expert systems and robotic process automation, for example, are transparent in how they do their work, but neither is capable of learning and improving. Deep learning, on the other hand, is great at learning from large volumes of labeled data, but it's almost impossible to understand how it creates the models it does. This "black box" issue can be problematic in highly regulated industries such as financial services, in which regulators insist on knowing why decisions are made in a certain way.

We encountered several organizations that wasted time and money pursuing the wrong technology for the job at hand. But if they're armed with a good understanding of the different technologies, companies are better positioned to determine which might best address specific needs, which vendors to work with, and how quickly a system can be implemented. Acquiring this understanding requires ongoing research and education, usually within IT or an innovation group.

In particular, companies will need to leverage the capabilities of key employees, such as data scientists, who have the statistical and big-data skills necessary to learn the nuts and bolts of these technologies. A main success factor is your people's willingness to learn. Some will leap at the opportunity, while others will want to stick with tools they're familiar with. Strive to have a high percentage of the former.

If you don't have data science or analytics capabilities in-house, you'll probably have to build an ecosystem of external service providers in the near term. If you expect to be implementing longer-term AI projects, you will want to recruit expert in-house talent. Either way, having the right capabilities is essential to progress.

Given the scarcity of cognitive technology talent, most organizations should establish a pool of resources—perhaps in a centralized function such as IT or strategy—and make experts available to high-priority projects throughout the organization. As needs and talent proliferate, it may make sense to dedicate groups to particular business functions or units, but even then a central coordinating function can be useful in managing projects and careers.

2. Creating a Portfolio of Projects

The next step in launching an AI program is to systematically evaluate needs and capabilities and then develop a prioritized portfolio of projects. In the companies we studied, this was usually done in workshops or through small consulting engagements. We recommend that companies conduct assessments in three broad areas.

Identifying the opportunities

The first assessment determines which areas of the business could benefit most from cognitive applications. Typically, they are parts of the company where "knowledge"—insight derived from data analysis or a collection of texts—is at a premium but for some reason is not available.

- **Bottlenecks.** In some cases, the lack of cognitive insights is caused by a bottleneck in the flow of information; knowledge exists in the organization, but it is not optimally distributed. That's often the case in health care, for example, where knowledge tends to be siloed within practices, departments, or academic medical centers.

- **Scaling challenges.** In other cases, knowledge exists, but the process for using it takes too long or is expensive to scale. Such is often the case with knowledge developed by financial advisers. That's why many investment and wealth management firms now offer AI-supported "robo-advice" capabilities that provide clients with cost-effective guidance for routine financial issues.

In the pharmaceutical industry, Pfizer is tackling the scaling problem by using IBM's Watson to accelerate the laborious process of drug-discovery research in immuno-oncology, an emerging approach to cancer treatment that uses the body's immune system to help fight cancer. Immuno-oncology drugs can take up to 12 years to bring to market. By combining a sweeping literature review with Pfizer's own data, such as lab reports, Watson is helping researchers to surface relationships and find hidden patterns that should speed the identification of new drug targets, combination therapies for study, and patient selection strategies for this new class of drugs.

- **Inadequate firepower.** Finally, a company may collect more data than its existing human or computer firepower can adequately analyze and apply. For example, a company may have massive amounts of data on consumers' digital behavior but lack insight about what it means or how it can be strategically applied. To address this, companies are using machine learning to support tasks such as programmatic buying of personalized digital ads or, in the case of Cisco Systems and IBM, to create tens of thousands of "propensity models" for determining which customers are likely to buy which products.

Determining the use cases

The second area of assessment evaluates the use cases in which cognitive applications would generate substantial value and contribute to business success. Start by asking key questions such as: How critical to your overall strategy is addressing the targeted problem? How difficult would it be to implement the proposed AI solution—both technically and organizationally? Would the benefits from launching the application be worth the effort? Next, prioritize the use cases according to which offer the most short- and long-term value, and which might ultimately be integrated into a broader platform or suite of cognitive capabilities to create competitive advantage.

Selecting the technology

The third area to assess examines whether the AI tools being considered for each use case are truly up to the task. Chatbots and intelligent agents, for example, may frustrate some companies because most of them can't yet match human problem solving beyond simple scripted cases (though they are improving rapidly). Other technologies, like robotic process automation that can streamline simple processes such as invoicing, may in fact slow down more-complex production systems. And while deep learning visual recognition systems can recognize images in photos and videos, they require lots of labeled data and may be unable to make sense of a complex visual field.

In time, cognitive technologies will transform how companies do business. Today, however, it's wiser to take incremental steps with the currently available technology while planning for transformational change in the not-too-distant future. You may ultimately want to turn customer interactions over to bots, for example, but for now it's probably more feasible—and sensible—to automate your internal IT help desk as a step toward the ultimate goal.

3. Launching Pilots

Because the gap between current and desired AI capabilities is not always obvious, companies should create pilot projects for cognitive applications before rolling them out across the entire enterprise.

Proof-of-concept pilots are particularly suited to initiatives that have high potential business value or allow the organization to test different technologies at the same time. Take special care to avoid "injections" of projects by senior executives who have been influenced by technology vendors. Just because executives and boards of directors may feel pressure to "do something cognitive" doesn't mean you should bypass the rigorous piloting process. Injected projects often fail, which can significantly set back the organization's AI program.

If your firm plans to launch several pilots, consider creating a cognitive center of excellence or similar structure to manage them. This approach helps build the needed technology skills and capabilities within the organization, while also helping to move small pilots into broader applications that will have a greater impact. Pfizer has more than 60 projects across the company that employ some form of cognitive technology; many are pilots, and some are now in production.

At Becton, Dickinson, a "global automation" function within the IT organization oversees a number of cognitive technology pilots that use intelligent digital agents and RPA (some work is done in partnership with the company's Global Shared Services organization). The global automation group uses end-to-end process maps to guide implementation and identify automation opportunities. The group also uses graphical "heat maps" that indicate the organizational activities most amenable to AI interventions. The company has successfully implemented intelligent agents in IT support processes, but as yet is not ready to support large-scale enterprise processes, like order-to-cash. The health insurer Anthem has developed a similar centralized AI function that it calls the Cognitive Capability Office.

Business-process redesign

As cognitive technology projects are developed, think through how workflows might be redesigned, focusing specifically on the division of labor between humans and the AI. In some cognitive projects, 80% of decisions will be made by machines and 20% will be made by humans; others will have the opposite ratio. Systematic redesign of workflows is necessary to ensure that humans and machines augment each other's strengths and compensate for weaknesses.

The investment firm Vanguard, for example, has a new "Personal Advisor Services" (PAS) offering, which combines automated investment advice with guidance from human advisers. In the new system, cognitive technology is used to perform many of the traditional tasks of investment advising, including constructing a customized portfolio, rebalancing portfolios over time, tax loss harvesting, and tax-efficient investment selection. Vanguard's human advisers serve as "investing coaches," tasked with answering investor questions, encouraging healthy financial behaviors, and being, in Vanguard's words, "emotional circuit breakers" to keep investors on plan. Advisers are encouraged to learn about behavioral finance to perform these roles effectively. The PAS approach has quickly gathered more than $80 billion in assets under management, costs are lower than those for purely human-based advising, and customer satisfaction is high. (See the exhibit "One company's division of labor.")

One company's division of labor

Vanguard, the investment services firm, uses cognitive technology to provide customers with investment advice at a lower cost. Its Personal Advisor Services system automates many traditional tasks of investment advising, while human advisers take on higher-value activities. Here's how Vanguard redesigned its work processes to get the most from the new system.

Cognitive technology	Adviser
Generates a financial plan	Understands investment goals
Provides goals-based forecasting in real time	Customizes an implementation plan
Rebalances portfolio to target mix	Provides investment analysis and retirement planning
Minimizes taxes	Develops retirement income and Social Security drawdown strategies
Tracks aggregated assets in one place	
Engages clients virtually	Serves as a behavioral coach
	Monitors spending to encourage accountability
	Offers ongoing wealth and financial-planning support
	Addresses estate-planning considerations

Source: Vanguard Group

Vanguard understood the importance of work redesign when implementing PAS, but many companies simply "pave the cow path" by automating existing work processes, particularly when using RPA technology. By automating established workflows, companies can quickly implement projects and achieve ROI—but they forgo the opportunity to take full advantage of AI capabilities and substantively improve the process.

Cognitive work redesign efforts often benefit from applying design-thinking principles: understanding customer or end-user needs, involving employees whose work will be restructured, treating designs as experimental "first drafts," considering multiple alternatives, and explicitly considering cognitive technology capabilities in the design process. Most cognitive projects are also suited to iterative, agile approaches to development.

4. Scaling Up

Many organizations have successfully launched cognitive pilots, but they haven't had as much success rolling them out organization-wide. To achieve their goals, companies need detailed plans for scaling up, which requires collaboration between technology experts and owners of the business process being automated. Because cognitive technologies typically support individual tasks rather than entire processes, scale-up almost always requires integration with existing systems and processes. Indeed, in our survey, executives reported that such integration was the greatest challenge they faced in AI initiatives.

Companies should begin the scaling-up process by considering whether the required integration is even possible or feasible. If the application depends on special technology that is difficult to source, for example, that will limit scale-up. Make sure your business process owners discuss scaling considerations with the IT organization before or during the pilot phase: An end run around IT is unlikely to be successful, even for relatively simple technologies like RPA.

The health insurer Anthem, for example, is taking on the development of cognitive technologies as part of a major modernization of its existing systems. Rather than bolting new cognitive apps onto legacy technology, Anthem is using a holistic approach that maximizes the value being generated by the cognitive applications, reduces the overall cost of development and integration, and creates a halo effect on legacy systems. The company is also redesigning processes at the same time to, as CIO Tom Miller puts it, "use cognitive to move us to the next level."

In scaling up, companies may face substantial change-management challenges. At one U.S. apparel retail chain, for example, the pilot project at a small subset of stores used machine learning for online product recommendations, predictions for optimal inventory and rapid replenishment models, and—most difficult of all—merchandising. Buyers, used to ordering product on the basis of their intuition, felt threatened and made comments like "If you're going to trust this, what do you need me for?" After the pilot, the buyers went as a group to the chief merchandising officer and requested that the program be killed. The executive pointed out that the results were positive and warranted expanding the project. He assured the buyers that, freed of certain merchandising tasks, they could take on more high-value work that humans can still do better than machines, such as understanding younger customers' desires and determining apparel manufacturers' future plans. At the same time, he acknowledged that the merchandisers needed to be educated about a new way of working.

If scale-up is to achieve the desired results, firms must also focus on improving productivity. Many, for example, plan to grow their way into productivity—adding customers and transactions without adding staff. Companies that cite head count reduction as the primary justification for the AI investment should ideally plan to realize that goal over time through attrition or from the elimination of outsourcing.

The Future Cognitive Company

Our survey and interviews suggest that managers experienced with cognitive technology are bullish on its prospects. Although the early successes are relatively modest, we anticipate that these technologies will eventually transform work. We believe that companies that are adopting AI in moderation now—and have aggressive implementation plans for the future—will find themselves as well positioned to reap benefits as those that embraced analytics early on.

Through the application of AI, information-intensive domains such as marketing, health care, financial services, education, and professional services could become simultaneously more valuable and less expensive to society. Business drudgery in every industry and function—overseeing routine transactions, repeatedly answering the same questions, and extracting data from endless documents—could become the province of machines, freeing up human workers to be more productive and creative. Cognitive technologies are also a catalyst for making other data-intensive technologies succeed, including autonomous vehicles, the Internet of Things, and mobile and multichannel consumer technologies.

The great fear about cognitive technologies is that they will put masses of people out of work. Of course, some job loss is likely as smart machines take over certain tasks traditionally done by humans. However, we believe that most workers have little to fear at this point. Cognitive systems perform tasks, not entire jobs. The human job losses we've seen were primarily due to attrition of workers who were not replaced or through automation of outsourced work. Most cognitive tasks currently being performed augment human activity, perform a narrow task within a much broader job, or do work that wasn't done by humans in the first place, such as big-data analytics.

Most managers with whom we discuss the issue of job loss are committed to an augmentation strategy—that is, integrating human and machine work, rather than replacing humans entirely. In our survey, only 22% of executives indicated that they considered reducing head count as a primary benefit of AI.

We believe that every large company should be exploring cognitive technologies. There will be some bumps in the road, and there is no room for complacency on issues of workforce displacement and the ethics of smart machines. But with the right planning and development, cognitive technology could usher in a golden age of productivity, work satisfaction, and prosperity.

Originally published in January–February 2018. Reprint R1801H

Stitch Fix's CEO on Selling Personal Style to the Mass Market

by Katrina Lake

AT STITCH FIX OUR BUSINESS MODEL IS SIMPLE: We send you clothing and accessories we think you'll like; you keep the items you want and send the others back. We leverage data science to deliver personalization at scale, transcending traditional brick-and-mortar and e-commerce retail experiences. Customers enjoy having an expert stylist do the shopping for them and appreciate the convenience and simplicity of the service.

Of course, making something seem simple and convenient to consumers while working profitably and at scale is complex. It's even more complex in the fashion retail industry, which is crowded, fickle, and rapidly changing. Other apparel retailers attempt to differentiate themselves through the lowest price or the fastest shipping; we differentiate ourselves through personalization. Each Fix shipment, as we call it, is a box containing five clothing and accessory items we've chosen just for you. Those choices are based on information you and millions of others have given us—first in an extensive questionnaire you fill out when you sign up, and then in feedback you provide after each shipment.

Stitch Fix sold $730 million worth of clothing in 2016 and $977 million worth in 2017. One hundred percent of our revenue results directly from our recommendations, which are the core of our business. We have more than 2 million active clients in the United States, and we carry more than 700 brands. We're not upselling you belts that match that blouse you just added to your cart, or touting a certain brand because you've bought it before, or using browsing patterns to intuit that you might be shopping for a little black dress—all activities that have low conversion rates. Instead we make unique and personal selections by combining data and machine learning with expert human judgment.

Data science isn't woven into our culture; it *is* our culture. We started with it at the heart of the business, rather than adding it to a traditional organizational structure, and built the company's algorithms around our clients and their needs. We employ more than 80 data scientists, the majority of whom have PhDs in quantitative fields such as math, neuroscience, statistics, and astrophysics. Data science reports directly to me, and Stitch Fix wouldn't exist without data science. It's that simple.

Not a Valley Story

We're far from the prototypical Silicon Valley start-up. I don't consider myself a serial entrepreneur: Stitch Fix is the first company I've launched. But I'm fascinated by retail experiences and how untouched they were by modern technology in the 21st century. During my undergraduate years at Stanford, in the early 2000s, and in my first job, as a consultant at the Parthenon Group, I did a lot of work with retailers and restaurants. While I loved both industries and how meaningful they were to people, I was intrigued that they still provided fundamentally the same experience they had in the 1970s—or even the 1950s—despite how much the world had changed. I wondered how they might adapt, and I wanted to be part of that future.

I moved on from Parthenon to become an associate at Leader Ventures, a VC firm, just as the iPhone appeared, in 2007. Still, I was

Idea in Brief

Lake's experience as a consultant to retailers and restaurants led to a fascination with how untouched those industries were by 21st-century technology. As a lover of both clothes and data, she felt certain that data could create a better experience with apparel—as long as the human element was preserved.

From the beginning Lake planned to build a data science operation to make Stitch Fix scalable. The company's revenue is dependent on great recommendations from its algorithm, so its data scientists have a direct line to the CEO. Data science

is deeply ingrained in the company culture: In addition to client recommendations of clothing, algorithms keep capital costs low, inventory moving, and deliveries efficient. Product development has adapted algorithms from genetics to find successful "traits" in clothing. Stitch Fix has even used machine learning to design apparel.

But, Lake says, shopping is inherently a personal and human activity, which is why human stylists can alter or override the product assortment a styling algorithm delivers before the client receives a shipment.

thinking about retail. I studied the economics of Blockbuster during the rise of Netflix. On one side was a company that dominated physical store sales; on the other was a company that dominated sales without stores. It was the perfect case study. And I could see exactly when the scale tipped. Whenever Netflix hit about 30% market share, the local Blockbuster closed. The remaining 70% of customers then faced a decision: try Netflix or travel farther to get movies. More of them tried Netflix, putting more pressure on Blockbuster. Another store would close, and more customers would face that try-or-travel decision, in a downward spiral.

I recognized that other retailers might suffer Blockbuster's fate if they didn't rethink their strategy. For example, how would someone buy jeans 10 years down the road? I knew it wouldn't be the traditional model: go to six stores, pull pairs of jeans off the racks, try them all on. And I didn't think it would resemble today's e-commerce model either: You have 15 tabs open on your browser while you check product measurements and look for what other shoppers are saying. Then you buy multiple pairs and return the ones that don't fit.

The part of me that loves data knew it could be used to create a better experience with apparel. After all, fit and taste are just a bunch of attributes: waist, inseam, material, color, weight, durability, and pattern. It's all just data. If you collect enough, you'll get a pretty good picture of what clothes people want.

But the part of me that loves clothes recognized the human element in shopping—the feeling of finding something you weren't expecting to and delighting in the fact that it fits you and your budget. I saw an opportunity to combine those two elements—data and human experience—to create a new model for buying clothes.

A Bad Idea?

At first I didn't plan to start a company; I was going to join a startup that wanted to pursue this idea. At Leader, I met with hundreds of entrepreneurs, hoping the right one would come through. That didn't happen. So I enrolled at Harvard Business School to pursue my risk-averse path to entrepreneurship. I used those two years to plan and launch my company. I received a term sheet to fund Stitch Fix in February 2011; I shipped the first Fix boxes from my apartment in April; and I graduated in May.

Not many people thought it was a good idea. One of my professors called it an inventory nightmare. I wanted to own all the inventory so that I could deeply understand each item and turn it into a lot of structured data. In retail, owning all the inventory is scary, and the professor thought it would make my strategy capital-intensive and risky. But the strategy was ultimately right. Using data to better understand what people want enables us to turn over inventory faster than many conventional retailers do, because we can buy the right things and get them to the right people. Selling inventory fast enough to pay vendors with cash from clients turns out to be a very capital-efficient model.

Then there were skeptical venture capitalists. I would come to pitch meetings with a box of clothes and a personalized card from the stylist. I remember that at one meeting, a VC said within the first five minutes, "I just don't understand why anyone would ever want to receive anything like this." I appreciated his honesty. Many of them were unexcited about warehouses full of clothes. Others were baffled that we employed human stylists who were paid hourly—a very un-VC idea at a time when everything was about automation and apps. Despite our early success, Series B funding conversations got a tepid response. "I think you're great, your team is amazing, and your business is working," one VC told me. "But I get to pick one or two boards a year, and I want to pick ones I feel connected to. I can't get passionate about retail or women's dresses."

That's fair—and frustrating. As it happens, 87% of the employees, 35% of the data scientists, and 32% of the engineers at Stitch Fix are women. More than 90% of venture capitalists are men, and I felt the industry's gender dynamic was working against us. In the end, what didn't kill us made us stronger, because it forced us to focus on profitability and capital efficiency. We've since used cash from our operations to launch new businesses, including men's apparel and plus sizes for women.

Finally, there was the industry itself. By making revenue dependent on fashion recommendations, I had picked one of the more difficult tasks for machine learning. Even people who think they're undiscerning about the clothes they wear do in fact care. Fit, style, material—these matter to all of us. It's a nuanced business. That makes it especially interesting but also more difficult. Early on, focus groups asserted that they just didn't believe we could pick out clothes they'd like. They'd say, "How will it work? Nothing will fit."

The idea of paying us a $20 styling fee up front, credited to your purchase if you keep something, also gave pause. Focus group participants would ask, "Why would I pay $20 when I don't get to pick anything out?" We needed customers to trust that they'd want to keep items. And that has turned out to be true—because of the data science.

Enter the Algorithms

When I started, my "data science" was rudimentary. I used Survey-Monkey and Google Docs along with some statistical methods to track preferences and try to make good recommendations. In the

Mix and Match

STITCH FIX USES DATA that clients supply—beginning with a "style profile"—and a suite of algorithms to capture their reactions to merchandise. Human stylists (algorithmically matched with clients) review and revise every box of five items before it is mailed. Clients respond with written answers to five survey questions about each item, along with comments. That feedback, together with purchase history, allows Stitch Fix to improve its picks over time.

The following illustrates how the algorithm and the stylist together might choose one client's very first Fix and two successive ones.

X Returned   ✔ Bought

Fix 1

The client's style profile guided both the algorithm's choice of this shirt and the stylist's choice of pale pink. ✔

The stylist approved the algorithm's choice of this all-season top, even though it's out of the stated price range, because the client likes florals. ✔

These slip-on sneakers have a high match rate among clients looking for a casual shoe. The stylist thought the floral pattern would add originality. ✔

The client asked for skinny jeans. The stylist selected green from among the algorithm's denim recommendations. **X**

Because the client's style profile said she loves textures, the stylist chose this studded blouse. **X**

---

beginning, I was essentially acting as a personal stylist. Sometimes I even delivered a Fix box in person. But my plan was always to build a data science operation that would make the business scalable. Our recommendations work because our algorithms are good, but our algorithms are good because data science underpins the company.

Three things make machine learning integral:

Data science reports to the CEO

At most companies, data science reports to the CTO, as part of the engineering team, or sometimes even to finance. Here it's separate, and we have a chief algorithms officer, Eric Colson, who has a seat

Fix 2

The client was looking for a versatile top. The algorithm identified this cashmere sweater because it has been extremely successful with women of her age and physical dimensions. ✔

The client did not like the fit of the green jeans, so the algorithm found a pair that fit better, and the stylist chose blue denim. **X**

The client loved the lightweight floral top in the previous box, so the stylist found this more vibrant variation, which the algorithm suggested would fit well. ✔

The client also loved the pink shirt in the previous box, so the stylist found a different take within the same color palette. ✔

The client wanted a new bag, and the algorithm found this one trending among women of her age. The stylist picked light green to pop against the red palette of the tops in the box. **X**

Fix 3

Because the client kept the cashmere sweater from the previous Fix, the stylist thought this piece, a little bolder, was worth taking a risk on. ✔

The algorithm chose this popular coat for its versatility and affordability. ✔

Stitch Fix now knows the client's preferred color and fit for jeans, so the stylist felt confident in exceeding her price range with this pair. ✔

The algorithm recommended this blouse because the client responded warmly to the color palette in the previous Fix. ✔

The stylist knows that the client is single and dating, so she chose these playful heels to dress up the skinny jeans. ✔

at the strategy table. Eric came from Netflix in August 2012. Before that he was an adviser to us. He became interested in our company because it presented a challenge. At Netflix, he recalls, someone said, "What if we just started playing a movie we think someone will like when they open the app?" That seemed like a bold but risky idea—to go all in on just one recommendation. He realized that's what Stitch Fix does. As an adviser, he found himself spending a vacation playing with some of our data. He decided to join us full-time—a huge coup for a little start-up.

Because our revenue is dependent on great recommendations from our algorithms, it's even more crucial that our data scientists have a direct line to the CEO. We also believe it sends a message to the organization as a whole about our values and our approach to strategy: Data science is extremely important, and other teams, such as marketing and engineering, will increase their capabilities by partnering closely with our data science team.

Innovation is done by data science

We've developed dozens of algorithms that no one ever asked for, because we allow our data science team to create new solutions and determine whether they have potential. No one explicitly asked the team to develop algorithms to do rebuy recommendations, for example. (Rebuys happen when a certain inventory item is selling well and we need to acquire more of it.) Our algorithms help us see these trends earlier and more accurately, so we can stock inventory more efficiently and be ready for spikes in demand. Recently the team came up with a way to track the movements of employees in our warehouses and created an algorithm that could help optimize routes without expensive remapping of the spaces as they change.

It's sometimes hard for people to imagine how deeply ingrained data science is in our culture. We use many kinds of algorithms now, and we're building many more. Personalized recommendations of clothing, of course, are driven by machine learning. Fulfillment and inventory management use algorithms to keep capital costs low, inventory moving, and deliveries efficient. Product development has adapted some algorithms from genetics to find successful "traits" in clothes. We've even started using machine learning to design apparel.

Hybrid Designs, our in-house clothing brand, came to life one rainy afternoon when a couple of data scientists were thinking about how to fill product gaps in the marketplace. For example, many female clients in their mid-40s were asking for capped-sleeve blouses, but that style was missing from our current inventory set. Fast-forward a year, and we have 29 apparel items for women and plus sizes that were designed by computer and meet some specific, previously unfilled needs our clients have.

Another way we apply a quantitative approach to fashion is with measurement data. We track anywhere from 30 to 100 measurements on a garment, depending on what type it is, and we now know—from the experiences of more than 2 million active clients—what kind of fit would make a customer spend outside her or his comfort zone. We know the optimal ratio of chest size to shirt width on a men's shirt. Using data analysis, we adjusted the distance from the collar to the first button on shirts for men with large chests. We know what proportion of the population fits a 27-inch inseam, and we can stock according to that proportion.

But in some ways, that's the easy part. The real challenge is having the right dress in the right color and the right size at the right time. The math around that is complex. We must account for all the measurements plus the taste of the customer, the season, the location, past trends—lots of variables.

Given a dollar to invest in the company and the choice to use it for marketing, product, or data science, we'd almost always choose data science. We're glad we started with data science at our core rather than trying to transform a traditional retailer, which I believe wouldn't have worked. For a traditional retailer to say, "Let's do what Stitch Fix does" would be like my saying, "I'd like to be taller now."

Don't forget the people

The analytical part of me loves our algorithmic approach. But shopping is inherently a personal and human activity. That's why we insist on combining data with a human stylist who can alter or override the product assortment our styling algorithm has delivered. Our stylists come from a range of design and retail backgrounds, but they all have an appreciation for the data and feel love and empathy for our clients. Humans are much better than machines at some things—and they are likely to stay that way for a long time.

For example, when a client writes in with a very specific request, such as "I need a dress for an outdoor wedding in July," our stylists immediately know what dress options might work for that event. In addition, our clients often share intimate details of a pregnancy, a major weight loss, or a new job opportunity—all occasions whose importance a machine can't fully understand. But our stylists know exactly how special such life moments are and can go above and beyond to curate the right look, connect with the clients, and improvise when needed. That creates incredible brand loyalty.

It's simple: A good person plus a good algorithm is far superior to the best person or the best algorithm alone. We aren't pitting people and data against each other. We need them to work together. We're not training machines to behave like humans, and we're certainly not training humans to behave like machines. And we all need to acknowledge that we're fallible—the stylist, the data scientist, me. We're all wrong sometimes—even the algorithm. The important thing is that we keep learning from that.

Originally published in May–June 2018. Reprint R1803A

Algorithms Need Managers, Too

by Michael Luca, Jon Kleinberg, and Sendhil Mullainathan

MOST MANAGERS' JOBS involve making predictions. When HR specialists decide whom to hire, they're predicting who will be most effective. When marketers choose which distribution channels to use, they're predicting where a product will sell best. When VCs determine whether to fund a start-up, they're predicting whether it will succeed. To make these and myriad other business predictions, companies today are turning more and more to computer algorithms, which perform step-by-step analytical operations at incredible speed and scale.

Algorithms make predictions more accurate—but they also create risks of their own, especially if we do not understand them. High-profile examples abound. When Netflix ran a million-dollar competition to develop an algorithm that could identify which movies a given user would like, teams of data scientists joined forces and produced a winner. But it was one that applied to DVDs—and as Netflix's viewers transitioned to streaming movies, their preferences shifted in ways that didn't match the algorithm's predictions.

Another example comes from social media. Today many sites deploy algorithms to decide which ads and links to show users. When these algorithms focus too narrowly on maximizing user click-throughs, sites become choked with low-quality "click-bait" articles. Click-through rates rise, but overall customer satisfaction may plummet.

Problems like these aren't inevitable. In our work designing and implementing algorithms and identifying new data sources with a range of organizations, we have seen that the source of difficulty often isn't bugs in the algorithms; it's bugs in the way we interact with them. To avoid missteps, managers need to understand what algorithms do well—what questions they answer and what questions they do not.

Why Do Smart Algorithms Lead Us Astray?

As a growing body of evidence shows, humanizing algorithms makes us more comfortable with them. This can be useful if, for example, you're designing an automated call function. A real person's voice is more likely than an electronic voice to get people to listen. The fundamental problem, however, is that people treat algorithms and the machines that run them the same way they'd treat an employee, supervisor, or colleague. But algorithms behave very differently from humans, in two important ways:

Algorithms are extremely literal

In the latest Avengers movie, Tony Stark (also known as Iron Man) creates Ultron, an artificial-intelligence defense system tasked with protecting Earth. But Ultron interprets the task literally, concluding that the best way to save Earth is to destroy all humans. In many ways, Ultron behaves like a typical algorithm: It does exactly what it's told—and ignores every other consideration. We get into trouble when we don't manage algorithms carefully.

The social media sites that were suddenly swamped with clickbait fell into a similar trap. Their overall goal was clear: Provide content that would be most appealing and engaging to users. In communicating it to the algorithm, they came up with a set of instructions that seemed like a good proxy—find items that users will click on the most. And it's not a bad proxy: People typically click on content because it interests them. But making selections solely on

Idea in Brief

The Problem

Algorithms are essential tools for planning, but they can easily lead decision makers astray.

The Causes

All algorithms share two characteristics: They're literal, meaning that they'll do exactly what you ask them to do. And they're black boxes, meaning that they don't explain why they offer particular recommendations.

The Solution

When formulating algorithms, be explicit about all your goals. Consider long-term implications of the data you examine. And make sure you choose the right data inputs.

the basis of clicks quickly filled sites with superficial and offensive material that hurt their reputation. A human would understand that the sites' designers meant "Maximize quality as measured by clicks," not "Maximize clicks even at the expense of quality." An algorithm, on the other hand, understands only what it is explicitly told.

Algorithms are black boxes

In Shakespeare's *Julius Caesar,* a soothsayer warns Caesar to "beware the ides of March." The recommendation was perfectly clear: Caesar had better watch out. Yet at the same time it was completely incomprehensible. Watch out for what? Why? Caesar, frustrated with the mysterious message, dismissed the soothsayer, declaring, "He is a dreamer; let us leave him." Indeed, the ides of March turned out to be a bad day for the ruler. The problem was that the soothsayer provided *incomplete* information. And there was no clue to what was missing or how important that information was.

Like Shakespeare's soothsayer, algorithms often can predict the future with great accuracy but tell you neither what will cause an event nor why. An algorithm can read through every *New York Times* article and tell you which is most likely to be shared on Twitter without necessarily explaining why people will be moved to tweet about it. An algorithm can tell you which employees are most likely to succeed without identifying which attributes are most important for success.

Recognizing these two limitations of algorithms is the first step to managing them better. Now let's look at other steps you can take to leverage them more successfully.

Be Explicit About All Your Goals

Everyone has objectives and directives, but we also know that the end doesn't always justify the means. We understand that there are soft (often unspoken) goals and trade-offs. We may turn down a little profit today for a gain in reputation tomorrow. We may strive for equality—even if it causes organizational pain in the short term. Algorithms, on the other hand, will pursue a specified objective single-mindedly. The best way to mitigate this is to be crystal clear about everything you want to achieve.

If you care about a soft goal, you need to state it, define it, and quantify how much it matters. To the extent that soft goals are difficult to measure, keep them top of mind when acting on the results from an algorithm.

At Google (which has funded some of our research on other topics), a soft-goal problem emerged with an algorithm that determines which ads to display. Harvard professor Latanya Sweeney unearthed it in a study. She found that when you typed names that were typically African American, like "Latanya Farrell," into Google, you were shown ads offering to investigate possible arrest records, but not when you searched on names like "Kristen Haring." Google's hard goal of maximizing clicks on ads had led to a situation in which its algorithms, refined through feedback over time, were in effect defaming people with certain kinds of names. It happened because people who searched for particular names were more likely to click on arrest records, which led these records to appear even more often, creating a self-reinforcing loop. This probably was not the intended outcome, but without a soft goal in place, there was no mechanism to steer the algorithm away from it.

We recently saw the importance of soft goals in action. One of us was working with a West Coast city to improve the efficiency of its restaurant inspections. For decades, the city had been doing them mostly at random but giving more-frequent scrutiny to places with prior violations. Choosing which establishments to inspect is an ideal job for an algorithm, however. Our algorithm found many more variables—not just past violations—to be predictive. The result was that the health department could identify probable offenders more easily and then find actual violations with far fewer inspections.

The officials loved the idea of making the process more efficient and wanted to move toward implementation. We asked if there were any questions or concerns. After an awkward silence, one person raised her hand. "I don't know how to bring this up," she said. "But there's an issue we should discuss." She explained that in some neighborhoods with tighter quarters, there tended to be more violations. These neighborhoods also happened to be home to higher percentages of minority residents with lower incomes. She did not want these neighborhoods to be excessively targeted by the algorithm. She was expressing a soft goal related to fairness. Our simple solution was to incorporate that objective into the algorithm by setting a ceiling on the number of inspections within each area. This would achieve the hard goal, identifying the restaurants most likely to have problems, while still respecting the soft one, ensuring that poor neighborhoods were not singled out.

Notice the extra step that allowed us to bake in soft goals: giving everyone an opportunity to articulate any concerns. We find that people often formulate soft goals as concerns, so asking for them explicitly facilitates more open and fruitful discussion. It's also critical to give people license to be candid and up-front—to say things that they wouldn't normally. This approach can surface a variety of issues, but the ones we see most commonly relate to fairness and to the handling of sensitive situations.

With a core objective and a list of concerns in hand, the designer of the algorithm can then build trade-offs into it. Often that may mean extending the objective to include multiple outcomes, weighted by importance.

Minimize Myopia

A popular consumer packaged goods company was purchasing products cheaply in China and selling them in the United States. It selected these products after running an algorithm that forecast which ones would sell the most. Sure enough, sales took off and cruised along nicely—until several months later, when customers started to return the items.

As it happens, the surprisingly high and steady return rate could have been predicted (even though the algorithm had failed to foresee it). The company obviously cared about quality, but it hadn't translated that interest into an algorithm that carefully projected consumer satisfaction; instead it had asked the algorithm to focus narrowly on sales. Ultimately, the company's new approach was to become great at forecasting not just how well products would sell but also how much people would enjoy and keep their products. The firm now looks for offerings that customers will rave about on Amazon and other platforms, and the product return rate has plummeted.

This company ran into a common pitfall of dealing with algorithms: Algorithms tend to be myopic. They focus on the data at hand—and that data often pertains to short-term outcomes. There can be a tension between short-term success and long-term profits and broader corporate goals. Humans implicitly understand this; algorithms don't unless you tell them to.

This problem can be solved at the objective-setting phase by identifying and specifying long-term goals. But when acting on an algorithm's predictions, managers should also adjust for the extent to which the algorithm is consistent with long-term aims.

Myopia is also the underlying weakness of programs that produce low-quality content by seeking to maximize click-throughs. The algorithms are optimizing for a goal that can be measured in the moment—whether a user clicks on a link—without regard to the longer-range and more important goal of keeping users satisfied with their experience on the site.

Nearsightedness can similarly be an issue with marketing campaigns. Consider a run-of-the-mill Gap advertising campaign with

Google. It would most likely lead to a spike in visits to Gap.com—because Google's algorithm is good at predicting who will click on an ad. The issue is, the real goal is increasing sales—not increasing website visits. To address this, advertising platforms can collect sales data through a variety of channels, such as partnerships with payment systems, and incorporate it into their algorithms.

What's more, website visits are a short-term behavior, whereas the long-term impact of advertisements includes the downstream effects on brand image and repeat business. While perfect data on such effects is hard to find, careful data audits can help a lot. Managers should systematically list all internal and external data that may be relevant to the project at hand. With a Google campaign, the Gap's marketers could begin by laying out all their objectives—high sales, low returns, good reputation, and so on—and then spell out ways to measure each. Product returns, online reviews, and searches for the term "Gap" would all be great metrics. The best algorithm could then build predictions from a combination of all these features, calibrating for their relative importance.

Choose the Right Data Inputs

Let's return to the example of health departments that are trying to identify restaurants at risk for causing foodborne illness. As mentioned earlier, cities historically have inspected either randomly or on the basis of prior inspection results. Working with Yelp, one of us helped the city of Boston use online reviews to determine which restaurants were most likely to violate local health codes, creating an algorithm that compared the text in reviews with historical inspection data. By applying it, the city identified the same number of violations as usual, but with 40% fewer inspectors—a dramatic increase in efficiency.

This approach worked well not just because we had a lot of restaurants to look at but because Yelp reviews provided a great set of data—something cities hadn't given much thought to. A Yelp review contains many words and a variety of information. The data is also diverse, because it's drawn from different sources. In short, it's quite unlike the inspector-created data cities were accustomed to working with.

When choosing the right data resources, keep in mind the following:

Wider is better

One trap companies often fall into is thinking of big data as simply a lot of records—for example, looking at one million customers instead of 10,000. But this is only half the picture. Imagine your data organized into a table, with a row for each customer. The number of customers is the length of the table. The amount you know about each customer determines the width—how many features are recorded in each row. And while increasing the length of the data will improve your predictions, the full power of big data comes from gathering wide data. Leveraging comprehensive information is at the heart of prediction. Every additional detail you learn about an outcome is like one more clue, and it can be combined with clues you've already collected. Text documents are a great source of wide data, for instance; each word is a clue.

Diversity matters

A corollary to this is that data should be diverse, in the sense that the different data sources should be relatively unrelated to one another. This is where extra predictive power comes from. Treat each data set like a recommendation from a friend. If the data sets are too similar, there won't be much marginal gain from each additional one. But if each data set has a unique perspective, a lot more value is created.

Understand the Limitations

Knowing what your algorithm can't tell you is just as important as knowing what it can. It's easy to succumb to the misguided belief that predictions made in one context will apply equally well in another. That's what prevented the 2009 Netflix competition from yielding more benefit to the company: The algorithm that accurately forecast which DVD a person would want to order in the mail wasn't nearly as good at pinpointing which movie a person would want to stream right now. Netflix got useful insights and good publicity from the contest, but the data it collected on DVDs did not apply to streaming.

Algorithms use existing data to make predictions about what might happen with a slightly different setting, population, time, or question. In essence, you're transferring an insight from one context to another. It's a wise practice, therefore, to list the reasons why the algorithm might not be transferable to a new problem and assess their significance. For instance, a health-code violation algorithm based on reviews and violations in Boston may be less effective in Orlando, which has hotter weather and therefore faces different food safety issues.

Also remember that correlation still doesn't mean causation. Suppose that an algorithm predicts that short tweets will get retweeted more often than longer ones. This does not in any way suggest that you should shorten your tweets. This is a prediction, not advice. It works as a prediction because there are many other factors that correlate with short tweets that make them effective. This is also why it fails as advice: Shortening your tweets will not necessarily change those other factors.

Consider the experiences of eBay, which had been advertising through Google for years. EBay saw that people who viewed those ads were more likely to shop at it than people who did not. What it didn't see was whether the advertisements (which were shown millions of times) were causing people to come to its site. After all, the ads were deliberately shown to likely eBay shoppers. To separate correlation from causation, eBay ran a large experiment in which it randomly advertised to some people and not others. The result? It turns out that the advertisements were for the most part useless, because the people who saw them already knew about eBay and would have shopped there anyway.

Algorithms capable of making predictions do not eliminate the need for care when drawing connections between cause and effect; they are not a replacement for controlled experiments. But what they can do is extremely powerful: identifying patterns too subtle to be detected by human observation, and using those patterns to generate accurate insights and inform better decision making. The challenge for us is to understand their risks and limitations and, through effective management, unlock their remarkable potential.

Originally published in January–February 2016. Reprint R1601H

Marketing in the Age of Alexa

by Niraj Dawar

THE AUTONOMOUS CAR *dropped Lori at her home and then left for its scheduled service at the dealership. It would be back in time to take her to the airport the next morning. On the way into her house, Lori gathered the drone deliveries from the drop box on her stoop. The familiar voice of Eve, a next-generation smart assistant like Alexa, greeted her in the foyer and gently reminded her of the travel plans for her upcoming conference in LA. Lori hadn't bothered to learn the details, since Eve had taken care of finding the best flight, seat, and hotel room that her company's expense policy would allow.*

As she unpacked her grocery delivery, Lori saw that Eve had adjusted her weekly purchases, omitting perishables and adding travel-size toiletries and sunblock. Calculating that Lori was running low on detergent (and aware she'd be coming home with laundry to do), the bot had ordered more but switched to a new, less expensive brand that was getting good consumer reviews. And, knowing that Lori wouldn't want to cook, it had arranged for her favorite takeout to be delivered upon her return.

Thank goodness for Eve, Lori thought to herself. In addition to managing her shopping and travel, the bot tracked her spending and kept her costs down. Each quarter, for example, Eve checked all the telecommunications plans on the market and compared them against Lori's projected data usage. Her current plan gave her the best price for her mostly evening and weekend usage, but with her brother's 40th birthday approaching, Eve had anticipated a lot of data traffic among Lori's friends and family and found a deal from an upstart firm that would save her money. That offer was instantly matched by Lori's current provider, a company that had paid to be featured on Eve and to have the right to meet competitors' prices. Lori relied on Eve for similar help with buying insurance, banking, and investment products, too. Sometimes she had to instruct her bot about her criteria and the trade-offs she was willing to make (for example, to forgo higher returns for a greener investment portfolio), but more recently, Eve had begun figuring out what product attributes she was after—even aesthetic ones— without having to be told.

Lori didn't know how she had ever coped without Eve. She had come to trust the bot not just for advice on complex purchases but also to make many of her routine decisions and to introduce her to new products and services she didn't even know she wanted.

Does This Scenario Sound Far-Fetched?

It isn't: All the technologies that Lori uses to interact with her world are either currently in development or already available—and being rapidly refined. Amazon, Google, Baidu, and other tech giants have launched artificial intelligence platforms with increasingly skilled digital assistants. While none have yet attained Eve's sweeping capabilities, that is clearly their goal—and it's just a matter of time before they get there.

AI assistants are rapidly colonizing consumers' homes. Analysts estimate that Amazon, for instance, has sold some 25 million Echo smart speakers, which people use to engage with its AI assistant, Alexa, and that number is expected to more than double by 2020. Once you take into account the millions of other devices that can already host Alexa through iOS or Android apps, Alexa's market penetration looks even higher.

Google Assistant, accessed chiefly through Google Home cylinders and Pixel phones, is now available on 400 million devices. Earlier this year Apple launched a Siri-enabled HomePod, and Samsung has acquired Viv, an intelligent assistant company founded by

Idea in Brief

The New Environment

Over the next decade, smart assistants like Alexa will transform how companies sell to and satisfy consumers, and global firms will battle to establish the preferred artificial intelligence platform.

The Changing Behavior

AI assistants will become trusted advisers to consumers, anticipating and satisfying their needs, ensuring that routine purchases flow uninterrupted to their households like electricity, and guiding them through complex buying decisions.

The Strategic Response

Brands will need to shift the focus of their marketing from consumers to AI platforms, seeking to influence platforms in order to get preferential positioning on AI assistants.

Siri's creators, to bolster its Bixby AI assistant platform. Microsoft and Tencent have platforms for their own AI assistants (Cortana and Xiaowei), and virtual assistants Chumenwenwen and Xiaoice (which is capable of uncannily human conversations and reportedly has 40 million registered users) are already popular in China.

Over the next decade, as these firms and others fight to establish the preferred consumer AI platform, AI assistants will transform how companies connect with their customers. They'll become the primary channel through which people get information, goods, and services, and marketing will turn into a battle for their attention.

AI assistants will help consumers navigate their increasingly overwhelming number of choices. Every year people buy from thousands of product categories, deciding among dozens or hundreds of options in each. Even routine purchases can be time-consuming; nonroutine purchases often require sorting through the nuances of competing offers and are fraught with risk. While shopping for shoes may be fun, picking the right toothbrush from more than 200 products is pretty tedious. Choosing the wrong tennis racket can ruin your game, and buying an ill-considered cell phone plan or insurance policy can be costly.

AI assistants will not only minimize costs and risks for consumers but also offer them unprecedented convenience. They'll ensure that routine purchases flow uninterrupted to households—just as water and electricity do now—and manage the complexity of more-involved shopping decisions by learning consumers' criteria and optimizing whatever trade-offs people are willing to make (such as a higher price for more sustainability).

The effects on the business landscape will be far-reaching. Technologies that revolutionize the way consumers interact with a marketplace also tend to reconfigure its dynamics and reshape the companies that sell into it. In the 1950s, for instance, the rise of supermarkets made scale and mass media much more important to marketers, triggering a wave of consolidation among consumer goods companies. AI platforms and assistants will likewise change the game for brands and retailers, altering the relative power of players in the value chain and the underlying basis of competition.

These predictions grow out of our ongoing research into the ways technology has been redefining relationships among customers, brands, and firms. In the course of it, we have reviewed hundreds of relevant academic, industry, and news articles, and held in-depth discussions and structured interviews with industry experts and executives at Google, L'Oréal, EURid, and other global businesses. (Ivey Business School graduate student assistants Gobind deep Singh and Vivek Astvansh helped us with the early literature reviews.) In this article we'll outline in more detail the near-term changes we expect AI platforms to bring about and explain the implications they hold for marketing strategy.

Marketing on Platforms

Once the dust settles, we expect that just a handful of general-purpose AI platforms will be left standing. (See the sidebar "The Coming Platform Shakeout.") Most consumers will use only one, whose assistant will be incorporated into their homes, cars, and mobile devices. The platform will gather and deliver information, and the assistant will be the consumer's interface with home systems, appliances, and other machines. The assistant will also be the portal to an infinite shopping mall of goods and services. The more

The Coming Platform Shakeout

TODAY THERE ARE PERHAPS A DOZEN SERIOUS CONTENDERS in the nascent AI platform industry. But we expect that this field will eventually be narrowed down to only a few. What will drive this concentration, and how will winners be chosen?

For starters, the market has high barriers to entry. Large general-purpose AI platforms are extremely expensive to build and run. It took thousands of engineers several years to develop Amazon's Alexa, for instance. Besides committing vast internal resources to development, each player must establish an extensive ecosystem of providers that supply data, services, skills, and apps. To succeed, platforms need a large installed base and a wide range of capabilities. Those that achieve scale and scope will have a natural advantage: The more a platform can do reliably and well, the more loyal users will be to it. Over time it will learn consumers' preferences and habits, which will make it even better at anticipating and satisfying people's needs, which will make consumers use it more. Those dynamics, combined with a lack of data portability across platforms, will make AI platforms sticky. Advantages will accrue mostly to just a few large platforms. While smaller platforms such as Uber's or Expedia's may coexist for a time, we expect they'll ultimately be incorporated into the large general platforms as vendors or as specific AI assistant skills.

consumers use a platform, the better it will understand their habits and preferences, and the better it will meet their needs—increasing their satisfaction in a self-reinforcing cycle.

Marketers' current obsession with creating an omnichannel customer experience will fade as AI platforms become a powerful marketing medium, sales and distribution channel, and fulfillment and service center—all rolled into one. The concentration of those functions within a few platforms will give their owners enormous clout, and branded products will find themselves in a weaker position. Consumer companies that feel that large retailers like Walmart wield too much power today will be even more alarmed by the might of AI platforms. As a major—or even primary—means of communicating with consumers, and the repository of reams of data about their habits, preferences, and consumption, the platforms will have a lot of influence over prices and promotions and the consumer relationship itself.

Brands today owe their success to their ability to signal quality and win buyers' loyalty. But in a world of AI platforms, marketers may find that consumers like Lori shift their allegiance from trusted brands to a trusted AI assistant. The activities that help brands cement relationships with buyers over time—understanding and filling people's needs, assuring quality, and consistently putting consumers' interests at the center—will in many cases be performed better by AI. In fact, we predict that AI assistants will win consumers' trust and loyalty better than any previous marketing technology. We therefore expect the focus of many brands to shift from reinforcing direct relationships with consumers to optimizing their positions on AI platforms. However, in selected cases it may still make strategic sense for brands to maintain strong ties with consumers outside the platforms. (See the sidebar "Will Brands Matter?")

These changes will have an impact on companies at three critical levels: customer acquisition, satisfaction, and retention.

Acquisition

With consumer data now being used to create finely targeted marketing, customer acquisition has become ever more efficient. Still, marketers' aim is far from perfect. Ads continue to be directed at consumers who aren't good prospects—and don't reach everyone who may be interested in an offering. Even when an ad does find the right audience, its message is often blunted by consumers' cognitive limitations: People might need to see the ad many times before it registers or may forget it entirely. They may remember only the parts that interest them (for example, the humor) but not the product's name or distinctive promise.

Those problems will matter less in the coming years, when the main target of the billions in annual spending on brand marketing will shift from forgetful, biased consumers to AI platforms that retain every last bit of information. Platforms will analyze that data, taking into account products' pricing, characteristics, past performance, and reviews (weighted by authenticity and relevance) and the consumers' preferences and past behavior. Customer acquisition will

Will Brands Matter?

THANKS TO AI PLATFORMS, the job of branded-goods companies is about to get much harder. Increasingly, AI assistants like Alexa will control access to those firms' customers, and brand recognition will play less of a role in product selection than dynamic and idiosyncratic AI algorithms will. That doesn't mean, though, that brands will no longer matter. They can respond in three ways:

First, they must invest aggressively in understanding the algorithms platforms use to recommend and choose products, including how they weight each brand for each consumer. In some categories and for some consumers, brands may be more important than price (Apple is an example). In others (say, toothbrushes), brands may be less relevant. AI algorithms will take such differences into consideration.

Second, brands should assess the value of maintaining direct ties with consumers. For some kinds of offerings, such as smart, connected consumer electronics, promoting brand awareness and loyalty outside AI platforms may be a good strategy. Smart products give companies a direct channel for communicating with customers and collecting data on them, which may make those companies less reliant on AI platforms. In such cases, ongoing investments in brand building will make sense.

Finally, while consumers are increasingly buying online, most purchases—currently about 90% of global retail sales—occur in brick-and-mortar stores. For the foreseeable future, consumers will continue to shop offline, where brands will remain influential. As consumers' purchasing shifts to AI platforms, brands should regularly evaluate how important the physical retail channels remain (that will vary widely by category) and adjust their strategy accordingly. Brands will still be the experts in the product categories in which they operate, with deep knowledge about consumer behavior and product innovation.

become even more of a science and will focus on a single channel—the platform—rather than on multiple channels.

In this universe, influencing the platforms' algorithms will be the key to winning. It will be crucial for companies to understand the customized purchasing criteria that the AI applies on behalf of each consumer. Sellers will probably have to pay platforms to get that information—and to be "listed" on them, in much the same way that brands now pay shelving fees to brick-and-mortar retailers. Marketers can also expect to bid on or otherwise pay extra for preferential positions, just as hotels today bid to appear at the top of the results on Expedia, or marketers compete in Google's AdWords auctions to come up first in searches. Though Amazon says it has no plans to add advertising to Alexa, CNBC has reported that the company is talking with several consumer goods firms about promoting their products on the platform. Experiments "in the works," said CNBC, would allow Alexa to make product recommendations based on a user's previous inquiries ("How do I clean grass stains?") or past shopping behavior. We believe that product placement and recommendations on AI platforms are inevitable and will, in time, be a major source of revenue.

In different ways, all these payments will be for access to the consumer. Companies will essentially reallocate to the platforms what they spend today on advertising, listing and slotting fees, and retail commissions. Brands will shape their offers and innovation strategies around getting AI assistants to showcase their products.

The bustling ecosystem that now helps companies woo customers, including ad agencies and media buyers, will need to learn to market through AI platforms. Marketing services that target platforms will be even more accountable than media buyers are today and will need to show links to actual consumer behavior. Traditional market research may be supplanted altogether by the intelligence about consumers' actual behavior that brands will be able to buy directly from platforms.

Satisfaction

Customer satisfaction drives loyalty, word of mouth, market share, and profitability. No wonder marketers are fixated on monitoring it. Imagine, then, a world where reliable satisfaction data is easier to get from AI platforms than from consumers themselves.

A platform serves consumers by constantly anticipating their needs. To do that it must collect granular data on their purchasing patterns and product use and try to understand their goals: Do they want food products to improve their health, energy products to minimize their environmental impact, and financial products to increase their long-term returns? Or are their criteria taste, price, and short-term performance? Sophisticated AI platforms will go further and figure out the trade-offs consumers are willing to make: How much more will they pay for a more healthful product? How much room in a car will they sacrifice to get better fuel efficiency? AI platforms will even know whether consumers are likely to adapt their requirements in different contexts—for example, if a person on a diet will make an exception for dessert when celebrating.

Because of all this, AI platforms will be able to predict what combination of features, price, and performance is most appealing to someone at a given moment. Ultimately, AI assistants may be able to satisfy customers' needs better than the customers themselves can. Relatively primitive recommendation engines are already moving in this direction, suggesting books, movies, and music that consumers didn't know they would enjoy.

AI platforms will lead to more-efficient sorting and matching in the marketplace. Consumers who prefer the Four Seasons, for instance, will be unlikely to be offered reservations at a Trump hotel by their platforms. So brands will want to sharpen their positioning in ways that the platforms will register.

Retention

Marketers assume that repeat purchases indicate customer satisfaction and are a sign of brand loyalty. Yet many customers keep buying a product not because it delights them but because they can't be bothered to explore alternatives if a brand is performing adequately. Put simply, most people have better things to do than evaluate the ingredients of laundry detergents. An AI assistant, however, does not. It can regularly reassess all brands in any category, whether laptops or chewing gum, and recommend a new one that might serve the consumer better. Some consumers may even like to switch things up just for the sake of variety—so their assistants, being aware of that, will periodically recommend new products they might like.

That routine reevaluation of purchases will force incumbent brands to constantly justify their positions. But it will also open opportunities for challengers. Competition will get more intense.

Though incumbents will need to innovate to hang on to customers, they'll be able to buy information from platforms that will help them inhibit brand switching. If a brand knows that a consumer is likely to defect (say, because she has indicated a desire for change to her assistant), it can compute retention metrics in real time to see whether she's worth keeping. If she is, the brand can make her a customized offer that reflects exactly what she needs to stay put. If the consumer accepts it, both she and the brand win: The brand keeps the business and the consumer gets a better deal. The AI platform is in the middle, serving both in ways that create value for each while generating revenue for itself.

On their part, challenger brands can use intelligence from a platform to acquire customers. Promotions through AI assistants will be the tool of choice for upstarts. Of course, once a challenger breaks in, it will be subject to threats from the incumbent and other rivals. The secret to competitive differentiation—and, hence, retention—will be constantly designing offers that meet a customer's evolving criteria. For brands, this will become as much a focus of innovation as developing better products is.

The Imperatives for Platforms

AI platforms will succeed only if consumers have faith in them. As one platform leader at Google told us, "Building trust will be the most important thing we do." To earn consumers' confidence, platforms must ensure three things: accuracy, alignment, and privacy.

Accuracy
By continually learning each individual's desires and requirements, the platform algorithms will hone their ability to please consumers. If a platform can recommend an alternative to a trusted brand that it thinks the consumer will like better, and the consumer is happier

How AI platforms create value

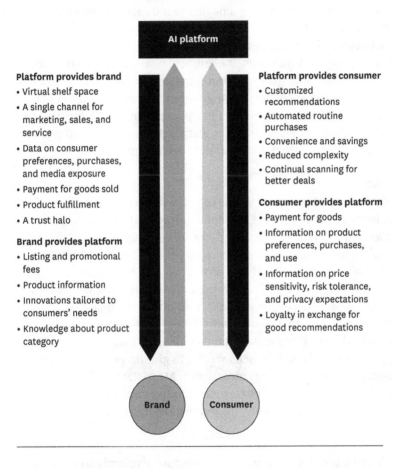

AI platform

Platform provides brand
- Virtual shelf space
- A single channel for marketing, sales, and service
- Data on consumer preferences, purchases, and media exposure
- Payment for goods sold
- Product fulfillment
- A trust halo

Brand provides platform
- Listing and promotional fees
- Product information
- Innovations tailored to consumers' needs
- Knowledge about product category

Platform provides consumer
- Customized recommendations
- Automated routine purchases
- Convenience and savings
- Reduced complexity
- Continual scanning for better deals

Consumer provides platform
- Payment for goods
- Information on product preferences, purchases, and use
- Information on price sensitivity, risk tolerance, and privacy expectations
- Loyalty in exchange for good recommendations

Brand

Consumer

with the alternative, that platform will supplant the brand as the object of her trust.

Alignment

There's a built-in conflict of interest that platforms must manage carefully. On one hand, they must single-mindedly focus on meeting consumers' needs; if they fall short, it will erode trust. On the other hand, they'll have contractual arrangements to provide preferred placements and consumer data to brands. If people sense that an assistant is pushing a paying brand that isn't aligned with their needs, that too will undermine trust. One solution might be for platforms to be transparent about their relationships with brands, just as Google is today when it identifies some search results as ads. Another may be to give paid and unpaid recommendations equal weight; if a consumer asks an AI assistant how best to remove grass stains, the response might include both a paying bleach and a comment that generic bleaches can be just as effective. The brand gets its plug, and the assistant demonstrates that it's trustworthy.

Privacy

Platform owners, as well as marketers, will need to strike a careful balance between the use of personal information and AI performance. The more data gathered, the more accurate the platform—but the more exposed consumers may feel. A solution here could be to offer customized privacy settings, as Facebook now does, giving users control over what information they share and how widely. Another, less satisfactory solution might be to argue, as Google sometimes does, that privacy is protected because consumer data is handled by machines without human intervention.

Consumers have long been willing to give up personal information, and even privacy, for convenience. AI assistants will offer much greater convenience but be far more intuitive and intrusive than any software now in use, greatly magnifying the trade-offs.

All consumer-facing firms can expect AI platforms to radically alter their relationships with customers. Their traditionally crucial assets, such as manufacturing capability and brands, will become less central as consumers' attention shifts to AI assistants, and the value of consumer data and AI's predictive ability soar. Push marketing (getting platforms to carry and promote a product) will become more important, while pull marketing (persuading consumers to seek products) becomes less so. The consumer

Three Questions for Brands

1. Whom Is the Platform Working For?

Before answering this question, let's apply it to traditional platforms. Consider credit card companies and brick-and-mortar retailers: Both perform functions—providing convenience, efficiency, and risk reduction—for the buyers and sellers they connect. AI platforms likewise work for multiple stakeholders, including brands. But bear in mind that if they don't serve the interests of the consumer, they won't be adopted. And the more consumers trust and rely on them, the more effective they are as a source of data and a channel for marketers. As with any well-functioning platform, creating value for parties on either side generates value for the platform itself.

2. What Do We Want from the Platform?

The obvious but incomplete answer is, we want it to sell our products. However, at the outset marketers should not think of a platform principally as a sales channel; they should look at it as a source of information. For a price, AI platforms will offer a view of consumer behavior and motivations more detailed than anything that's ever been available before. That nuanced understanding will allow companies to redesign every aspect of marketing—from segmentation to pricing to product features and promotional offers—to better meet consumers' needs. Platforms in turn will promote the improved products—and become the superior sales channel marketers seek.

3. How Can We Make Sure the Platform Chooses Us?

Here, brands will have two levers. One will be to pay for preferential positioning; the other, and likely the most powerful, will be to continually innovate their offerings so that they align with customers' stated and implicit needs, drawing on data supplied by the platforms. This will require brands to sharpen their differentiation; hone their ability to compete on speed, quality, and cost; and recognize and respond to rapid or subtle shifts in consumer tastes.

---

will remain the target of brand-building efforts, but marketing that encourages trial and repeat purchases will be more effective when aimed at AI. Though the marketplace will be more efficient, companies will encounter intense pressure to offer consumers the best deal—the one most closely aligned with the preferences identified by AI gatekeepers.

For a long time, consumer goods companies, used to maximizing economies of scale because of their large fixed investments in production and brands, have zeroed in on one strategic question: How much more of our product can we sell? AI platforms will present a very different opportunity: to maximize the depth of the relationship with the consumer by offering a wide range of products—in other words, economies of scope. Investments in building trust with consumers and their AI assistants will be amortized by asking, What else does this buyer need? Superior marketing strategy will still matter—firms must acquire, satisfy, and retain consumers in the AI world—but what it involves is likely to change substantially.

Originally published in May–June 2018. Reprint R1803E

Why Every Organization Needs an Augmented Reality Strategy

by Michael E. Porter and James E. Heppelmann

THERE IS A FUNDAMENTAL DISCONNECT between the wealth of digital data available to us and the physical world in which we apply it. While reality is three-dimensional, the rich data we now have to inform our decisions and actions remains trapped on two-dimensional pages and screens. This gulf between the real and digital worlds limits our ability to take advantage of the torrent of information and insights produced by billions of smart, connected products (SCPs) worldwide.

Augmented reality, a set of technologies that superimposes digital data and images on the physical world, promises to close this gap and release untapped and uniquely human capabilities. Though still in its infancy, AR is poised to enter the mainstream; according to one estimate, spending on AR technology will hit $60 billion in 2020. AR will affect companies in every industry and many other types of organizations, from universities to social enterprises. In the coming months and years, it will transform how we learn, make decisions, and interact with the physical world. It will also change how enterprises serve customers, train employees, design and create products, and manage their value chains, and, ultimately, how they compete.

In this article we describe what AR is, its evolving technology and applications, and why it is so important. Its significance will grow exponentially as SCPs proliferate, because it amplifies their power to create value and reshape competition. AR will become the new interface between humans and machines, bridging the digital and physical worlds. While challenges in deploying it remain, pioneering organizations, such as Amazon, Facebook, General Electric, Mayo Clinic, and the U.S. Navy, are already implementing AR and seeing a major impact on quality and productivity. Here we provide a road map for how companies should deploy AR and explain the critical choices they will face in integrating it into strategy and operations.

What Is Augmented Reality?

Isolated applications of AR have been around for decades, but only recently have the technologies required to unleash its potential become available. At the core, AR transforms volumes of data and analytics into images or animations that are overlaid on the real world. Today most AR applications are delivered through mobile devices, but increasingly delivery will shift to hands-free wearables such as head-mounted displays or smart glasses. Though many people are familiar with simple AR entertainment applications, such as Snapchat filters and the game Pokémon Go, AR is being applied in far more consequential ways in both consumer and business-to-business settings. For example, AR "heads-up" displays that put navigation, collision warning, and other information directly in drivers' line of sight are now available in dozens of car models. Wearable AR devices for factory workers that superimpose production-assembly or service instructions are being piloted at thousands of companies. AR is supplementing or replacing traditional manuals and training methods at an ever-faster pace.

More broadly, AR enables a new information-delivery paradigm, which we believe will have a profound impact on how data is structured, managed, and delivered on the internet. Though the web transformed how information is collected, transmitted, and

Idea in Brief

The Problem

While the physical world is three-dimensional, most data is trapped on 2-D screens and pages. This gulf between the real and digital worlds limits our ability to make the best use of the volumes of information available to us.

The Solution

Augmented reality solves this problem by superimposing digital images and data on real objects.

By putting information directly into the context in which we'll apply it, AR speeds our ability to absorb and act on it.

The Outcome

Pioneering organizations, including GE, Mayo Clinic, and the U.S. Navy, are using AR to improve productivity, quality, and training. By combining the strengths of humans and machines, AR will dramatically increase value creation.

accessed, its model for data storage and delivery—pages on flat screens—has major limits: It requires people to mentally translate 2-D information for use in a 3-D world. That isn't always easy, as anyone who has used a manual to fix an office copier knows. By superimposing digital information directly on real objects or environments, AR allows people to process the physical and digital simultaneously, eliminating the need to mentally bridge the two. That improves our ability to rapidly and accurately absorb information, make decisions, and execute required tasks quickly and efficiently.

AR displays in cars are a vivid illustration of this. Until recently, drivers using GPS navigation had to look at a map on a flat screen and then figure out how to apply it in the real world. To take the correct exit from a busy rotary, for example, the driver needed to shift his or her gaze between the road and the screen and mentally connect the image on the map to the proper turnoff. AR heads-up displays lay navigational images directly over what the driver sees through the windshield. This reduces the mental effort of applying the information, prevents distraction, and minimizes driver error, freeing people to focus on the road. (For more on this, see the sidebar "Enhancing Human Decision Making.")

Converging physical and digital

Augmented reality reduces the mental effort needed to connect digital information about the physical world with the context it applies to.

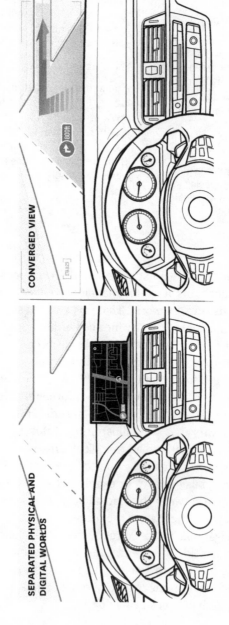

SEPARATED PHYSICAL AND DIGITAL WORLDS

Mentally transposing GPS images onto the road ahead is demanding and prone to errors.

CONVERGED VIEW

AR superimposes digital data directly on the real world.

Enhancing Human Decision Making

At its core, the power of augmented reality grows out of the way humans process information. We access information through each of our five senses—but at different rates. Vision provides us with the most information by far: An estimated 80% to 90% of the information humans get is accessed through vision.

The ability to absorb and process information is limited by our mental capacity. The demand on this capacity is referred to as "cognitive load." Each mental task we undertake reduces the capacity available for other, simultaneous tasks.

Cognitive load depends on the mental effort required to process a given type of information. For example, reading instructions from a computer screen and acting on them creates a greater cognitive load than hearing those same instructions, because the letters must be translated into words and the words interpreted. Cognitive load also depends on "cognitive distance," or the gap between the form in which information is presented and the context in which it is applied. Consider what happens when someone refers to a smartphone for directions while driving. The driver must consume the information from the screen, retain that information in working memory, translate the directions into the physical environment in front of him, and then act on those directions, all while operating the vehicle. There is significant cognitive distance between the digital information on the screen and the physical context in which information is applied. Dealing with this distance creates cognitive load.

The combination of the speed at which information is transmitted and absorbed and the cognitive distance involved in applying it lies at the root of the much-repeated phrase "A picture is worth a thousand words." When we look at the physical world, we absorb a huge amount and variety of information almost instantaneously. By the same token, an image or picture that superimposes information on the physical world, placing it in context for us, reduces cognitive distance and minimizes cognitive load.

This explains why AR is so powerful. There is no better graphical user interface than the physical world we see around us when it is enhanced by a digital overlay of relevant data and guidance where and when they are needed. AR eliminates dependence on out-of-context and hard-to-process 2-D information on pages and screens while greatly improving our ability to understand and apply information in the real world.

AR is making advances in consumer markets, but its emerging impact on human performance is even greater in industrial settings. Consider how Newport News Shipbuilding, which designs and builds U.S. Navy aircraft carriers, uses AR near the end of its manufacturing process to inspect a ship, marking for removal steel construction structures that are not part of the finished carrier. Historically, engineers had to constantly compare the actual ship with complex 2-D blueprints. But with AR, they can now see the final design superimposed on the ship, which reduces inspection time by 96%—from 36 hours to just 90 minutes. Overall, time savings of 25% or more are typical for manufacturing tasks using AR.

AR's Key Capabilities

As we've previously explained (see "How Smart, Connected Products Are Transforming Competition," HBR, November 2014), the SCPs spreading through our homes, workplaces, and factories allow users to monitor product operations and conditions in real time, control and customize product operations remotely, and optimize product performance using real-time data. And in some cases, intelligence and connectivity allow SCPs to be fully autonomous.

AR powerfully magnifies the value created by those capabilities. Specifically, it improves how users visualize and therefore access all the new monitoring data, how they receive and follow instructions and guidance on product operations, and even how they interact with and control the products themselves.

Visualize

AR applications provide a sort of X-ray vision, revealing internal features that would be difficult to see otherwise. At the medical device company AccuVein, for instance, AR technology converts the heat signature of a patient's veins into an image that is superimposed on the skin, making the veins easier for clinicians to locate. This dramatically improves the success rate of blood draws and other vascular procedures. AR more than triples the likelihood of a successful needle stick on the first try and reduces the need for "escalations" (calling for assistance, for example) by 45%.

Bosch Rexroth, a global provider of power units and controls used in manufacturing, uses an AR-enhanced visualization to demonstrate the design and capabilities of its smart, connected CytroPac hydraulic power unit. The AR application allows customers to see 3-D representations of the unit's internal pump and cooling options in multiple configurations and how subsystems fit together.

Instruct and guide

AR is already redefining instruction, training, and coaching. These critical functions, which improve workforce productivity, are inherently costly and labor-intensive and often deliver uneven results. Written instructions for assembly tasks, for instance, are frequently hard and time-consuming to follow. Standard instructional videos aren't interactive and can't adapt to individual learning needs. In-person training is expensive and requires students and teachers to meet at a common site, sometimes repeatedly. And if the equipment about which students are being taught isn't available, they may need extra training to transfer what they've learned to a real-world context.

AR addresses those issues by providing real-time, on-site, step-by-step visual guidance on tasks such as product assembly, machine operation, and warehouse picking. Complicated 2-D schematic representations of a procedure in a manual, for example, become interactive 3-D holograms that walk the user through the necessary processes. Little is left to the imagination or interpretation.

At Boeing, AR training has had a dramatic impact on the productivity and quality of complex aircraft manufacturing procedures. In one Boeing study, AR was used to guide trainees through the 50 steps required to assemble an aircraft wing section involving 30 parts. With the help of AR, trainees completed the work in 35% less time than trainees using traditional 2-D drawings and documentation. And the number of trainees with little or no experience who could perform the operation correctly the first time increased by 90%.

AR-enabled devices can also transmit what an on-site user is seeing to a remote expert, who can respond with immediate guidance. In effect, this instantly puts the expert at the user's side, regardless of location. This capability not only improves worker performance but substantially reduces costs—as Lee Company, which sells and services building systems, has discovered. It uses AR to help its field technicians with installations and repairs. A remote expert can see what the tech is viewing through his or her AR device, guide the tech through the work to be done, and even annotate the tech's view with instructions. Getting expert support from a central location in real time has increased Lee's tech utilization dramatically. And, by reducing the number of repeat visits, Lee saves more than $500 per technician per month in labor and travel costs. The company calculates a return of $20 on every dollar invested in AR.

Interact

Traditionally, people have used physical controls such as buttons, knobs, and, more recently, built-in touchscreens to interact with products. With the rise of SCPs, apps on mobile devices have increasingly replaced physical controls and allowed users to operate products remotely.

AR takes the user interface to a whole new level. A virtual control panel can be superimposed directly on the product and operated using an AR headset, hand gestures, and voice commands. Soon, users wearing smart glasses will be able to simply gaze at or point to a product to activate a virtual user interface and operate it. A worker wearing smart glasses, for instance, will be able to walk a line of factory machines, see their performance parameters, and adjust each machine without physically touching it.

The interact capability of AR is still nascent in commercial products but is revolutionary. Reality Editor, an AR app developed by the Fluid Interfaces group at MIT's Media Lab, provides a glimpse of how it is rapidly evolving. Reality Editor makes it easy to add an interactive AR experience to any SCP. With it, people can point a smartphone or a tablet at an SCP (or, eventually, look at it through smart glasses), "see" its digital interfaces and the capabilities that can be programmed, and link those capabilities to hand gestures or voice commands or even to another smart product. For example, Reality Editor can allow a user to see a smart light bulb's controls for color and intensity and set up voice commands like "bright" and "mood" to activate them. Or different settings of the bulb can be linked to buttons on a smart light switch the user can place anywhere that's convenient.

The technologies underpinning these capabilities are still emerging, but the accuracy of voice commands in noisy environments is improving, and advances in gesture and gaze tracking have been rapid. GE has already tested the use of voice commands in AR experiences that enable factory workers to perform complex wiring processes in wind turbines—and has achieved a 34% increase in productivity.

Combining AR and Virtual Reality

AR's well-known cousin, virtual reality, is a complementary but distinct technology. While AR superimposes digital information on the physical world, VR replaces physical reality with a computer-generated environment. Though VR is used mostly for entertainment applications, it can also replicate physical settings for training purposes. It is especially useful when the settings involved are hazardous or remote. Or, if the machinery required for training is not available, VR can immerse technicians in a virtual environment using holograms of the equipment. So when needed, VR adds a fourth capability—simulate—to AR's core capabilities of visualize, instruct, and interact.

AR will be far more widely applied in business than VR will. But in some circumstances, combining AR and VR will allow users to transcend distance (by simulating faraway locations), transcend time (by reproducing historical contexts or simulating possible future situations), and transcend scale (by allowing users to engage with environments that are either too small or too big to experience directly). What's more, bringing people together in shared virtual environments can enhance comprehension, teamwork, communication, and decision making.

Ford, for example, is using VR to create a virtual workshop where geographically dispersed engineers can collaborate in real time on holograms of vehicle prototypes. Participants can walk around and go inside these life-size 3-D holograms, working out how to refine design details such as the position of the steering wheel, the angle of the dashboard, and the location of instruments and controls without having to build an expensive physical prototype and get everyone to one location to examine it.

The U.S. Department of Homeland Security is going a step further by combining AR instructions with VR simulations to train personnel in responding to emergency situations such as explosions. This reduces costs and—in cases in which training in real environments would be dangerous—risk. The energy multinational BP overlays AR training procedures on VR simulations that replicate specific drilling conditions, like temperature, pressure, topography, and ocean currents, and that instruct teams on operations and help them practice coordinated emergency responses to disasters without high costs or risk.

How AR Creates Value

AR creates business value in two broad ways: first, by becoming part of products themselves, and second, by improving performance across the value chain—in product development, manufacturing, marketing, service, and numerous other areas.

AR as a product feature

The capabilities of AR play into the growing design focus on creating better user interfaces and ergonomics. The way products convey important operational and safety information to users has increasingly become a point of differentiation (consider how mobile apps have supplemented or replaced embedded screens in products like Sonos audio players). AR is poised to rapidly improve such interfaces.

Dedicated AR heads-up displays, which have only recently been incorporated into automobiles, have been a key feature in elite military products, such as fighter jets, for years and have been adopted in commercial aircraft as well. These types of displays are too expensive and bulky to integrate into most products, but wearables such as smart glasses are a breakthrough interface with wide-ranging implications for all manufacturers. With smart glasses, a user can see an AR display on any product enabled to communicate with them.

If you view a kitchen oven through smart glasses, for example, you might see a virtual display that shows the baking temperature, the minutes remaining on the timer, and the recipe you are following. If you approach your car, an AR display might show you that it is locked, that the fuel tank is nearly full, and that the left-rear tire's pressure is low.

Because an AR user interface is purely software based and delivered via the cloud, it can be personalized and can continually evolve. The incremental cost of providing such an interface is low, and manufacturers also stand to save considerable amounts when traditional buttons, switches, and dials are removed. Every product manufacturer needs to carefully consider the disruptive impact that this next-generation interface may have on its offering and competitive positioning.

AR and the value chain

The effects of AR can already be seen across the value chain, but they are more advanced in some areas than in others. In general, visualize and instruct/guide applications are now having the greatest impact on companies' operations, while the interact capability is still emerging and in pilot testing.

Product development. Though engineers have been using computer-aided design (CAD) capabilities to create 3-D models for 30 years, they have been limited to interacting with those models through 2-D windows on their computer screens, which makes it harder for them to fully conceptualize designs. AR allows 3-D models to be superimposed on the physical world as holograms, enhancing engineers' ability to evaluate and improve designs. For example, a life-size 3-D hologram of a construction machine can be positioned on the ground, and engineers can walk around it, peer under and over it, and even go inside it to fully appreciate the sight lines and ergonomics of its design at full scale in its intended setting.

AR also lets engineers superimpose CAD models on physical prototypes to compare how well they match. Volkswagen is using this technique—which makes any difference between the latest design and the prototype visually obvious—to check alignment in digital design reviews. This improves the accuracy of the quality assurance process, in which engineers previously had to painstakingly compare 2-D drawings with prototypes, and makes it five to 10 times faster.

We expect that in the near future AR-enabled devices such as phones and smart glasses, with their embedded cameras, accelerometers, GPS, and other sensors, will increasingly inform product design by exposing when, where, and how users actually interact with the product—how often a certain repair sequence is initiated, for example. In this way the AR interface will become an important source of data.

Manufacturing. In manufacturing, processes are often complex, requiring hundreds or even thousands of steps, and mistakes are costly. As we've learned, AR can deliver just the right information the moment it's needed to factory workers on assembly lines, reducing errors, enhancing efficiency, and improving productivity.

In factories, AR can also capture information from automation and control systems, secondary sensors, and asset management systems and make visible important monitoring and diagnostic data about each machine or process. Seeing information such as efficiency and defect rates in context helps maintenance technicians understand problems and prompts factory workers to do proactive maintenance that may prevent costly downtime.

Iconics, which specializes in automation software for factories and buildings, has begun to integrate AR into its products' user interfaces. By attaching relevant information to the physical location where it will be best observed and understood, the AR interfaces enable more-efficient monitoring of machines and processes.

Logistics. Warehouse operations are estimated to account for about 20% of all logistics costs, while picking items from shelves represents up to 65% of warehouse costs. In most warehouses, workers still perform this task by consulting a paper list of things to collect and then searching for them. This method is slow and error-prone.

The logistics giant DHL and a growing number of other companies are using AR to enhance the efficiency and accuracy of the picking process. AR instructions direct workers to the location of each product to be pulled and then suggest the best route to the next product. At DHL this approach has led to fewer errors, more-engaged workers, and productivity gains of 25%. The company is now rolling out AR-guided picking globally and testing how AR can enhance other types of warehouse operations, such as optimizing the position of goods and machines in layouts. Intel is also using AR in warehouses and has achieved a 29% reduction in picking time, with error rates falling to near zero. And the AR application is allowing new Intel workers to immediately achieve picking speeds 15% faster than those of workers who've had only traditional training.

Marketing and sales. AR is redefining the concept of showrooms and product demonstrations and transforming the customer experience. When customers can see virtually how products will look or function in a real setting before buying them, they have more-accurate expectations, more confidence about their purchase decisions, and greater product satisfaction. Down the road, AR may even reduce the need for brick-and-mortar stores and showrooms altogether.

When products can be configured with different features and options—which can make them difficult and costly to stock—AR is a particularly valuable marketing tool. The construction products company AZEK, for instance, uses AR to show contractors and consumers how its decking and paver products look in various colors and arrangements. Customers can also see the simulations in context: If you look at a house through a phone or a tablet, the AR app can add a deck onto it. The experience reduces any uncertainty customers might feel about their choices and shortens the sales cycle.

In e-commerce, AR applications are allowing online shoppers to download holograms of products. Wayfair and IKEA both offer libraries with thousands of 3-D product images and apps that integrate them into a view of an actual room, enabling customers to see how furniture and decor will look in their homes. IKEA also uses its app to collect important data about product preferences in different regions.

After-sales service. This is a function where AR shows huge potential to unlock the value-creating capabilities of SCPs. AR assists technicians serving customers in the field in much the same way it helps workers in factories: by showing predictive analytics data generated by the product, visually guiding them through repairs in real time, and connecting them with remote experts who can help optimize procedures. For example, an AR dashboard might reveal to a field technician that a specific machine part will most likely fail within a month, allowing the tech to preempt a problem for the customer by replacing it now.

At KPN, a European telecommunications service provider, field engineers conducting remote or on-site repairs use AR smart glasses to see a product's service-history data, diagnostics, and location-based information dashboards. These AR displays help them make better decisions about how to resolve issues, producing an 11% reduction in overall costs for service teams, a 17% decrease in work-error rates, and higher repair quality.

Xerox used AR to connect field engineers with experts instead of providing service manuals and telephone support. First-time fix rates increased by 67%, and the engineers' efficiency jumped by 20%. Meanwhile, the average time it took to resolve problems dropped by two hours, so staffing needs fell. Now Xerox is using AR to connect remote technical experts directly with customers. This has increased by 76% the rate at which technical problems are resolved by customers without any on-site help, cutting travel costs for Xerox and minimizing downtime for customers. Perhaps not surprisingly, Xerox has seen its customer satisfaction rates rise to 95%.

Human resources. Early AR adopters like DHL, the U.S. Navy, and Boeing have already discovered the power of delivering step-by-step visual worker training on demand through AR. AR allows instruction to be tailored to a particular worker's experience or to reflect the prevalence of particular errors. For example, if someone repeatedly makes the same kind of mistake, he can be required to use AR support until his work quality improves. At some companies, AR has reduced the training time for new employees in certain kinds of work to nearly zero and lowered the skill requirements for new hires.

This is especially advantageous for the package delivery company DHL, which faces surges in demand during peak seasons and is heavily dependent on the effective hiring and training of temporary workers. By providing real-time training and hands-on guidance on navigating warehouses and properly packing and sorting materials, AR has reduced DHL's need for traditional instructors and increased the onboarding speed for new employees.

AR and Strategy

AR will have a widespread impact on how companies compete. As we've explained in our previous HBR articles, SCPs are changing the structure of almost all industries as well as the nature of competition within them—often expanding industry boundaries in the process. SCPs give rise to new strategic choices for manufacturers, ranging from what functionality to pursue and how to manage data rights and security, to whether to expand a company's scope of products and compete in smart systems.

The increasing penetration of AR, along with its power as the human interface with SCP technologies, raises some new strategic questions. While the answers will reflect each company's business and unique circumstances, AR will become more and more integral to every firm's strategy.

Here are the essential questions companies face:

1. What is the range of AR opportunities in the industry, and in what sequence should they be pursued? Companies must weigh AR's potential impact on customers, product capabilities, and the value chain.

2. How will AR reinforce a company's product differentiation? AR opens up multiple differentiation paths. It can create companion experiences that expand the capabilities of products, give customers more information, and increase product loyalty. AR interfaces that enhance products' functionality or ease of use can be big differentiators, as can those that substantially improve product support, service, and uptime. And AR's capacity to provide new kinds of feedback on how customers use products can help companies uncover further opportunities for product differentiation.

The right differentiation path will depend on a company's existing strategy; what competitors are doing; and the pace of technology advances, especially in hardware.

3. Where will AR have the greatest impact on cost reduction? AR enables new efficiencies that every firm must explore. As we've noted, it can significantly lower the cost of training, service, assembly, design, and other parts of the value chain. It can also substantially cut manufacturing costs by reducing the need for physical interfaces.

Each company will need to prioritize AR-driven cost-reduction efforts in a way that's consistent with its strategic positioning. Firms with sophisticated products will need to capitalize on AR's superior and low-cost interface, while many commodity producers will focus on operational efficiencies across the value chain. In consumer industries and retail, marketing-related visualize applications are the most likely starting point. In manufacturing, instruct applications are achieving the most immediate payoff by addressing inefficiencies in engineering, production, and service. And AR's interact capability, though still emerging, will be important across all industries with products that have customization and complex control capabilities.

4. Should the company make AR design and deployment a core strength, or will outsourcing or partnering be sufficient? Many firms are scrambling to access the digital talent needed for AR development, which is in short supply. One skill in great demand is user experience or user interface (UX/UI) design. It's critical to present 3-D digital information in ways that make it easy to absorb and act on; companies want to avoid making a stunning but unhelpful AR experience that defeats its core purpose. Effective AR experiences also require the right content, so people who know how to create and manage it—another novel skill—are crucial too. Digital modeling capabilities and knowledge of how to apply them in AR applications are key as well.

Over time we expect companies to create teams dedicated to AR, just as they set up such teams to build and run websites in the 1990s and 2000s. Dedicated teams will be needed to establish the infra-structure that will allow this new medium to flourish and to develop and maintain the AR content. Many firms have started to build AR skills in-house, but few have mastered them yet.

Whether to hire and train AR employees or partner with specialty software and services companies is an open question for many. Some companies have no choice but to treat AR talent as a strategic asset and invest in acquiring and developing it, given AR's poten-tially large impact on competition in their business. However, if AR is important but not essential to competitive advantage, firms can partner with specialty software and services companies to leverage outside talent and technology.

The challenges, time, and cost involved in building the full set of AR technologies we have described are significant, and specializa-tion always emerges in each component. In the early stages of AR, the number of technology and service suppliers has been limited, and companies have built internal capabilities. However, best-of-breed AR vendors with turnkey solutions are starting to appear, and it will become increasingly difficult for in-house efforts to keep up with them.

5. How will AR change communications with stakeholders? AR complements existing print and 2-D digital communication approaches and in some cases can replace them altogether. Yet we see AR as much more than just another communication channel. It is a fundamentally new means of engaging with people. Just consider the novel way it helps people absorb and act on information and instructions.

The web, which began as a way to share technical reports, ulti-mately transformed business, education, and social interaction. We expect that AR will do the same thing for communication—changing it in ways far beyond what we can envision today. Companies will need to think creatively about how they can use this nascent channel.

Deploying AR

AR applications are already being piloted and deployed in products and across the value chain, and their number and breadth will only grow.

Every company needs an implementation road map that lays out how the organization will start to capture the benefits of AR in its business while building the capabilities needed to expand its use. When determining the sequence and pace of adoption, companies must consider both the technical challenges and the organizational skills involved, which vary from context to context. Specifically, organizations need to address five key questions:

1. Which development capabilities will be required? Some AR experiences involve more complexity than others. Experiences that allow people to visualize products in different configurations or settings—like those created by IKEA, Wayfair, and AZEK—are a relatively easy place for companies to start. Consumers just need to be encouraged to download and launch AR apps, and only a mobile device is needed to use them.

Instruction applications, like the ones Boeing and GE employ in manufacturing, are more difficult to build and use. They require the capacity to develop and maintain dynamic 3-D digital content and often benefit greatly from the use of head-mounted displays or smart glasses, which are still in the early stages of development.

Apps that produce interactive experiences, which create significant value for both consumers and businesses, are the most challenging to develop. They also involve less-mature technology, such as voice or gesture recognition, and the need to integrate with software that controls SCPs. Most companies will start with static visualizations of 3-D models, but they should build the capability to move quickly into dynamic instructional experiences that have greater strategic impact.

2. How should organizations create digital content? Every AR experience, from the least to the most sophisticated, requires content. In some cases it's possible to repurpose existing digital content, such as product designs. Over time, however, more-complex, dynamic contextual experiences must be built from scratch, which requires specialized expertise.

Simple applications, such as an AR-enhanced furniture catalog, may need only basic product representations. More-sophisticated business instruction applications, however, such as those used for machine repair, will require accurate and highly detailed digital product representations. Companies can create these by adapting CAD models used in product development or by using digitization techniques such as 3-D scanning. The most sophisticated AR experiences also need to tap real-time data streams from enterprise business systems, SCPs, or external data sources and integrate them into the content. To prepare for broadening the AR portfolio, companies should take an inventory of existing 3-D digital assets in CAD and elsewhere and invest in digital modeling capabilities.

3. How will AR applications recognize the physical environment? To accurately superimpose digital information on the physical world, AR technologies must recognize what they're looking at. The simplest approach is to determine the location of the AR device using, say, GPS and show relevant information for that location without anchoring it to a specific object. This is known as an "unregistered" AR experience. Vehicle heads-up navigation displays typically work this way.

Higher-value "registered" experiences anchor information to specific objects. They can do this through markers, such as bar codes, logos, or labels, which are placed on the objects and scanned by the user with an AR device. A more powerful approach, however, uses technology that recognizes objects by comparing their shape to a catalog of 3-D models. This allows a maintenance technician, for example, to instantly recognize and interact with any type of equipment he or she is responsible for maintaining and to do so from any angle. While markers are a good starting point, shape-recognition technologies are advancing quickly, and organizations will need the capability to use them to tap into many of the highest-value AR applications.

4. What AR hardware is required? AR experiences aimed at broad consumer audiences have typically been designed for smartphones, taking advantage of their simplicity and ubiquity. For more-sophisticated experiences, companies use tablets, which offer larger screens, better graphics, and greater processing power. Since tablet penetration is lower, companies will often provide them to users. For certain high-value applications—notably those in aircraft and automobiles—manufacturers are building dedicated AR heads-up displays into their products—a costly approach.

Eventually, however, most AR applications for service, manufacturing, and even product interfaces will require head-mounted displays that free users' hands. This technology is currently both immature and expensive, but we expect that affordable smart glasses will become widely available in the next few years and will play a major part in releasing AR's full power. Microsoft, Google, and Apple now offer AR technologies optimized for their own devices. However, most organizations should take a cross-platform approach that allows AR experiences to be deployed across multiple brands of phones and tablets and should make sure they're ready for smart glasses when they arrive.

5. Should you use a software-development or a content-publishing model? Many early AR experiences have been delivered through stand-alone software applications that are downloaded, complete with digital content, to a phone or a tablet. This approach creates reliable, high-resolution experiences and allows organizations to make apps that don't require internet connectivity. The problem with this model is that any change to the AR experience requires software developers to rewrite the app, which can create expensive bottlenecks.

An emerging alternative uses commercial AR-publishing software to create AR content and host it in the cloud. The AR experience can then be downloaded on demand using a general-purpose app running on an AR device. Like website content, the AR content can be updated or supplemented without changing the software itself—an important benefit when large amounts of information and frequent content changes are involved. The content-publishing model will become common as more and more machines and products include real-time AR interaction and control. A content-publishing capability is essential to scaling AR up across the organization.

The Broader Impact

The digital revolution, with its SCPs and explosion of data, is unleashing productivity and unlocking value across the economy. Increasingly, the constraint is not a lack of data and knowledge but how to assimilate and act on them—in other words, the interface with humans. AR is emerging as a leading solution to this challenge.

At the same time, the rapid evolution of machine learning and automation is raising serious concerns about human opportunity. Will there be enough jobs for everyone, especially for people without advanced education and knowledge? In a world of artificial intelligence and robots, will humans become obsolete?

It is easy to conclude that new technology diminishes human opportunity. Yet new inventions have been replacing human labor for centuries, and they have led to growth in employment, not a decline. Technology has dramatically increased our productivity and our standard of living. It has given rise to new kinds of offerings that meet new needs and require new types of workers. Many of today's jobs involve products and services that did not even exist a hundred years ago. A lesson of history is that today's digital revolution will generate new waves of innovation and new kinds of work that we cannot yet imagine.

The role of humans in this future is misunderstood. People have unique strengths that machines and algorithms will not replicate anytime soon. We have sophisticated motor skills—well beyond what robots are capable of today—that allow us to do the subtle manipulation that's needed in, say, replacing a machine part or wiring a turbine. Even relatively less skilled work, such as drawing blood, pruning a garden, or repairing a flat tire, requires human dexterity and defies automation. Human cognition adapts instantaneously to novel situations; people easily adjust the way they interpret information, solve problems, exercise judgment, and take action to suit their circumstances. Humans have flexibility, imagination, intuition, and creative ability that for the foreseeable future are beyond the reach of any machine.

How Does Augmented Reality Work?

Augmented reality starts with a camera-equipped device—such as a smartphone, a tablet, or smart glasses—loaded with AR software. When a user points the device and looks at an object, the software recognizes it through computer vision technology, which analyzes the video stream.

The device then downloads information about the object from the cloud, in much the same way that a web browser loads a page via a URL. A fundamental difference is that the AR information is presented in a 3-D "experience" superimposed on the object rather than in a 2-D page on a screen. What the user sees, then, is part real and part digital.

AR can provide a view of the real-time data flowing from products and allow users to control them by touchscreen, voice, or gesture. For example, a user might touch a stop button on the digital graphic overlay within an AR experience—or simply say the word "stop"—to send a command via the cloud to a product. An operator using an AR headset to interact with an industrial robot might see superimposed data about the robot's performance and gain access to its controls.

As the user moves, the size and orientation of the AR display automatically adjust to the shifting context. New graphical or text information comes into view while other information passes out of view. In industrial settings, users in different roles, such as a machine operator and a maintenance technician, can look at the same object but be presented with different AR experiences that are tailored to their needs.

A 3-D digital model that resides in the cloud—the object's "digital twin"—serves as the bridge between the smart object and the AR. This model is created either by using computer-aided design, usually during product development, or by using technology that digitizes physical objects. The twin then collects information from the product, business systems, and external sources to reflect the product's current reality. It is the vehicle through which the AR software accurately places and scales up-to-date information on the object.

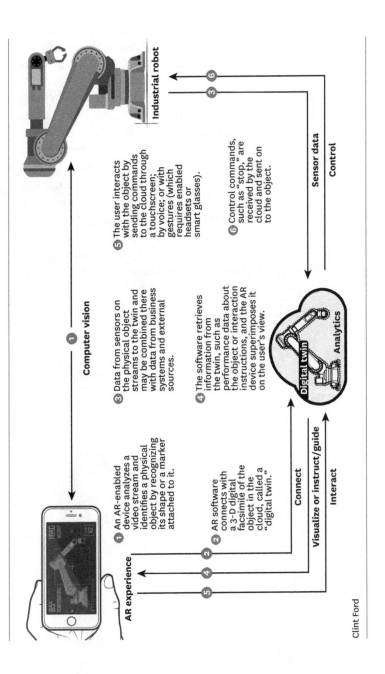

Computer vision

AR experience

Industrial robot

① An AR-enabled device analyzes a video stream and identifies a physical object by recognizing its shape or a marker attached to it.

② AR software connects with a 3-D digital facsimile of the object in the cloud, called a "digital twin."

③ Data from sensors on the physical object streams to the twin and may be combined there with data from business systems and external sources.

④ The software retrieves information from the twin, such as performance data about the object or interaction instructions, and the AR device superimposes it on the user's view.

⑤ The user interacts with the object by sending commands to the cloud through a touchscreen; by voice; or with gestures (which requires enabled headsets or smart glasses).

⑥ Control commands, such as "stop," are received by the cloud and sent on to the object.

Digital twin

Analytics

Connect

Visualize or instruct/guide

Interact

Sensor data

Control

Clint Ford

While the advances in artificial intelligence and robotics are impressive, we believe that combining the capabilities of machines with humans' distinctive strengths will lead to far greater productivity and more value creation than either could generate alone. What's needed to realize this opportunity is a powerful human interface that bridges the gap between the digital and physical worlds. We see AR as a historic innovation that provides this. It helps humans enhance their own capabilities by taking full advantage of new digital knowledge and machine capabilities. It will profoundly change training and skill development, allowing people to perform sophisticated work without protracted and expensive conventional instruction—a model that is inaccessible to so many today. AR, then, enables people to better tap into the digital revolution and all it has to offer.

Originally published in November–December 2017. Reprint R1706B

Drones Go to Work

by Chris Anderson

EVERY MORNING AT THE CONSTRUCTION SITE down the street from my office, the day starts with a familiar hum. It's the sound of the regular drone scan, when a small black quadcopter flies itself over the site in perfect lines, as if on rails. The buzz overhead is now so familiar that workers no longer look up as the aircraft does its work. It's just part of the job, as unremarkable as the crane that shares the air above the site. In the sheer normalness of this—a flying robot turned into just another piece of construction equipment—lies the real revolution.

"Reality capture"—the process of digitizing the physical world by scanning it inside and out, from the ground and the air—has finally matured into a technology that's transforming business. You can see it in small ways in Google Maps, where data is captured by satellites, airplanes, and cars, and presented in both 2-D and 3-D. Now that kind of mapping, initially designed for humans, is done at much higher resolution in preparation for the self-driving car, which needs highly detailed 3-D maps of cities in order to efficiently navigate. The methods of creating such models of the real world are related to the technology of "motion capture," which drives movies and video games today. Normally that requires bringing the production to the scanners—putting people in a large room outfitted for scanning and then creating the scene. But drones flip that, allowing us to bring the scanner to the scene. They're just regular cameras (and some smart software) precisely revolving around objects to create photo-realistic digital models.

In some ways it's astonishing that we're using drones on construction sites and in movies. Ten years ago the technology was still in labs. Five years ago it was merely very expensive. Today you can buy a drone at Walmart that can do real enterprise work, using software in the cloud. Now that it's so cheap and easy to put cameras in the sky, it's becoming commercially useful. Beyond construction, drone data is used in agriculture (crop mapping), energy (solar and wind turbine monitoring), insurance (roof scanning), infrastructure (inspection), communications, and countless other industries that touch the physical world. We know that "you can manage only what you can measure," but usually measuring the real world is hard. Drones make it much easier.

Industries have long sought data from above, generally through satellites or planes, but drones are better "sensors in the sky" than both. They gather higher-resolution and more-frequent data than satellites (whose view is obscured by clouds over two-thirds of the planet at any time), and they're cheaper, easier, and safer than planes. Drones can provide "anytime, anywhere" access to overhead views with an accuracy that rivals laser scanning—and they're just getting started. In this century's project to extend the internet to the physical world, drones are the path to the third dimension—up. They are, in short, the "internet of flying things."

You might think of drones as toys or flying cameras for the GoPro set, and that is still the lion's share of the business. But like the smartphone and other examples of the "commercialization of enterprise" before them, drones are now being outfitted with business-grade software and becoming serious data-collection platforms—hardware as open and extensible as a smartphone, with virtually limitless app potential. As in any app economy, surprising and ingenious uses will emerge that we haven't even thought of yet; and predictable and powerful apps will improve over time.

Or you might think of drones as delivery vehicles, since that's the application—consumer delivery—that the media grabs on to most ferociously when seeking click-generating amazing/scary visions of the future. Frankly, delivery is one of the least compelling, most complicated applications for drones (anything that involves

Idea in Brief

At breakneck speed, drones have moved from expensive military technology to toys for tech enthusiasts and now to tools for business. Hundreds of thousands of them are already in the sky, doing work. But if you are only thinking about little helicopters dropping off packages, you're not seeing the full potential of drones. Their real power is unleashed not by the hardware but by the software. Drones are a platform—less pilotless planes and more flying smartphones. The apps being created for them are varied and ingenious. Drones are disruptive. They change the equation on cost and labor for many operational tasks. From construction to mining to communications to media, companies are finding advantages to using drones, and another wave of innovation is coming as they progress from piloted to autonomous. It's time to understand the drone economy and develop a strategy.

autonomously flying in crowded environments is the black-diamond slope of technology and regulation). Most of the industry is focused on the other side of the continuum: on data, not delivery—commercial use over privately owned land, where the usual concerns about privacy, annoyance, and scary robots overhead are minimized.

Drone economics are classically disruptive. Already drones can accomplish in hours tasks that take people days. They can provide deeply detailed visual data for a tiny fraction of the cost of acquiring the same data by other means. They're becoming crucial in workplace safety, removing people from precarious processes such as cell-tower inspection. And they offer, literally, a new view into business: Their low-overhead perspective is bringing new insights and capabilities to fields and factories alike.

Like any robot, a drone can be autonomous, which means breaking the link between pilot and aircraft. Regulations today require that drones have an "operator" on the ground (even if the operation is just pushing a button on a smartphone and idly watching as the drone does its work). But as drones are getting smarter, regulators are starting to consider flights beyond "visual line of sight"—ones in which onboard sensors and machine vision will more than compensate for the eyes of a human on the ground far away. Once such fully autonomous use is allowed, the historic "one pilot/one air-craft" calculus can become "one operator/many vehicles" or even "*no* operator/many vehicles." That's where the real economic potential of autonomy will kick in: When the marginal cost of scanning the world approaches zero (because robots, not people, are doing the work), we'll do a lot more of it. Call this the "democratization of earth observation": a low-cost, high-resolution alternative to satellites. Anytime, anywhere access to the skies.

The drone economy is real, and you need a strategy for exploiting it. Here's how to think about what's happening—and what's going to happen. We'll start back at the construction site, a work environment in desperate need of what drones can provide.

Capturing Reality for the Cost of a Nice Lunch

The construction industry is the world's second largest (after agriculture), worth $8 trillion a year. But it's remarkably inefficient. The typical commercial construction project runs 80% over budget and 20 months behind schedule, according to McKinsey.

On-screen, in the architect's CAD file, everything looks perfect. But on-site, in the mud and dust, things are different. And the difference between concept and reality is where about $3 trillion of that $8 trillion gets lost, in a cascade of change orders, rework, and schedule slips.

Drones are meant to close that gap. The one buzzing outside my window, taking passes at the site, is capturing images with a high-performance camera mounted on a precision gimbal. It's taking regular photos (albeit at very high resolution), which are sent to the cloud and, using photogrammetry techniques to derive geometries from visual data, are turned into photo-realistic 2-D and 3-D models. (Google does the same thing in Google Maps, at lower resolution and with data that might be two or three years old. To see this, switch to Google Earth view and click on the "3-D" button.) In the construction site trailer, the drone's data shows up by mid-morning as an overhead view of the site, which can be zoomed in for detail the size of a U.S. quarter or rotated at any angle, like a video game or virtual reality scene. Superimposed on the scans are the CAD files used to guide the construction—an "as designed" view overlaid on an "as built" view. It's like an augmented reality lens into what should be versus what *is*, and the difference between the two can be worth thousands of dollars a day in cost savings on each site—billions across the industry. So the site superintendent monitors progress daily.

Mistakes, changes, and surprises are unavoidable whenever idealized designs meet the real world. But they can be minimized by spotting clashes early enough to fix them, work around them, or at least update the CAD model to reflect changes for future work. There are lots of ways to measure a construction site, ranging from tape measures and clipboards to lasers, high-precision GPS, and even X-rays. But they all cost money and take time, so they're not used often, at least not over the entire site. With drones, a whole site can be mapped daily, in high detail, for as little as $25 a day.

Rising from the Ground to Fill the Missing Middle

The ascent of the drone economy is a steep one. Ten years ago unmanned aerial vehicles were military technology, costing millions of dollars and cloaked in secrecy. But then came the smartphone, bringing with it a suite of component technologies, from sensors and fast processors to cameras, broadband wireless, and GPS. All those chips enabled the remarkable supercomputer in your pocket, but the economies of scale of smartphone production also made them cheap and available for other uses. The first step was to transform adjacent industries, including robotics. I call this proliferation of components "the peace dividend of the smartphone wars."

Companies including my own came out of this moment. Cheap high-powered components and a maker's attitude allowed enthusiasts and entrepreneurs to reimagine drones not as coming down from higher in the sky but as rising from the ground. Rather than seeing "airplanes without pilots," we saw "smartphones with propellers." Moving at the pace of the smartphone industry, not the aerospace industry, drones went from hackers' devices to hobbyists' instruments to toys costing less than $100 at your local big-box store in less than four years—perhaps the fastest transfer of technology from CIA to Costco in history. Five years ago the main commercial objection to the word "drone" was that it had military connotations. Now it's that people think of the aircraft as playthings. Has any word changed its meaning from "weapon" to "toy" faster?

And it doesn't end there. Wave one was technology, wave two was toys, and now comes the third and most important wave. Drones are becoming *tools*. The market for people who want flying selfie cameras may be limited, but the market for data about the physical world is as big as the world itself.

Drones are starting to fill the "missing middle" between satellites and street level, digitizing the planet in high resolution and near-real time at a tiny fraction of the cost of alternatives.

The trajectory of this third wave—drones as tools—is more dramatic than that of the two preceding waves. First drones will populate the skies in increasing numbers as regulations and technology allow safer use. Estimates vary widely; in 2018 approximately 100,000 operators are managing 200,000 drones, doing some work or another.

Next, the market for drone apps will explode as more and more people find ingenious uses. Drones will remain primarily data-collection vehicles, but the breadth of apps for them is only just beginning to be discovered. For example, drones have already been used for search and rescue and for wildlife monitoring. They can provide wireless internet access (something Facebook is investing in) and deliver medicine in the developing world. And they can not only map crops but also spray them with pesticides or deposit new seeds and beneficial insects.

Then, drones will gain even greater cost advantages when they don't just remove the pilot from the cockpit but remove the pilot entirely. The true breakthrough will come with autonomy.

Autonomous, Small, and Countless

Technology to allow drones to fly themselves exists and is improving quickly, going from simple GPS guidance to true visual navigation—the way a human would fly. Take humans out of the loop, and suddenly aircraft look more like the birds that inspired them: autonomous, small, and countless; born for the air and able to navigate it tirelessly and effortlessly. We are as yet tourists in the air, briefly visiting it at great cost. By breaking the link between man and machine, we can occupy the skies. The third dimension is the last frontier on Earth to be properly colonized (yes, both up to the skies and down under the seas, but we'll leave the latter to our aquatic-drone cousins). Colonize it we will, but as with space and the ocean depths, we'll use robots, not humans.

Why now? A combination of three trends. First, the price/performance bounty of the smartphone tech we talked about earlier made drones cheap and good. For example, the gyroscopic and other sensors packed into a tiny $3 chip in your phone were just a decade ago mechanical devices costing as much as $100,000 and mounted in enclosures ranging in size from lunch boxes to dorm fridges.

Second, the ability to make cheap and good drones put them within the reach of regular consumers (willing to spend up to $1,000) who had a real use case (aerial video and photography). As a result, companies had to make them easy to use—just swipe and fly—to drive adoption. Drones had to become more sophisticated as users became *less* sophisticated.

Third, once the consumer drone boom unexpectedly put more than a million drones—ranging from small toys to high-end "prosumer" models—into the skies over America in less than four years under a "recreational use" exemption to the FAA's strict rules about flying things, the regulators had to respond. To steer the market toward safer use without inhibiting it, the agency accelerated rules that would allow drones to be used commercially without the need for pilots' licenses or special waivers. The new rules took effect in August 2016, essentially kicking off the commercial drone era.

The Rise of Cloud Robotics

To this point we've focused mostly on drones themselves—the hardware, its cost and capabilities, and what we can attach to it to get work done. But when setting a drone strategy, it's important to think less about drones and more about apps. The hardware is primarily an empty vessel to fill with work to be done: taking photographs and video, scanning, moving objects, enabling communication.

And collecting data. More than anything, drones are collection vehicles. Their ability to amass data from a unique, valuable perspective (above, but not too far above) fast and at low cost makes them ideal collectors. Any drone strategy has to go beyond the drone to the data. And that means moving innovation to the cloud.

The history of modern Silicon Valley goes mostly like this:

1. Invent the personal computer.

2. Connect personal computers to local networks.

3. Connect local networks to the global internet.

4. Do all that again wirelessly.

5. Distribute computing and data throughout this network, from the apps in your pocket to massive computing clusters in the cloud.

6. Extend that beyond people to things, including moving things, linking as much of the world as possible into one interconnected network.

"Cloud robotics" is just the combination of the last two activities: connecting robots to the cloud so that both get smarter. That includes all robots—not just drones but also driverless cars, manufacturing and warehousing robots, and maybe someday robots in your home. But for now, we'll focus on drones.

The biggest change in drones (and in robotics—indeed, in electronics broadly) over the past decade is the *assumption of connectivity*. Unlike earlier generations of robots, which required bespoke communications systems, the robots that have come out of the smartphone industry inherited their "born connected" architecture.

Already it's hard to remember how things used to work: Amass data, then download it, then analyze it. No more. Data flows from source to device to analysis automatically and invisibly. Increasingly, it does what technology should always do: just work.

The implications of this shift are profound. When devices are designed from the ground up to be connected, three big things change:

1. The devices tend to get better over time, not worse

Unlike in the old stand-alone model, in which products start their march to obsolescence the moment they are made, connected devices get most of their features from their software, not their hardware, and that software can be updated, just like the software on your smartphone. Think of a Tesla, which gets new features automatically on an almost weekly basis. The technical term for such devices is "exotropic," and they tend to rise in value over time—unlike "entropic" devices, whose value tends to decline. Of course, the hardware has limits, and eventually even connected devices become obsolete. But the point is that rather than follow the traditional long decay slope from the point of purchase, connected devices improve in utility for as long as they can. In the case of drones, new abilities, from improved performance to new autonomous features, just appear overnight via "over the air" upgrades.

2. They have "outboard intelligence"

They're part of the internet of things—not the silly part, like connected lightbulbs, but the clever part (which, being clever, usually avoids the buzzwordy internet-of-things label). For example, Amazon Echo has enough intelligence in the box to harness immense intelligence in the cloud. It's not just a sensor for the internet but also a limb by which the internet can project into the physical world. For a drone, this means that it doesn't have to be programmed to scan a site using a standard path. Instead, it starts by taking a few pictures of the site, and then it uploads them to the cloud so that algorithms there can analyze them in real time and prepare a custom scan path that's just right for that site, on that day, with that lighting and those shadows. Think of this as *the data determining the mission, not the mission determining the data.*

3. They make the internet smarter too

Connected devices don't just get intelligence from the network; they feed data back to it. The current AI renaissance is due less to improved computation and algorithms than to the ability simply to access *vastly more data*. Much of that data, today and tomorrow, comes from measuring the world—both people and their environments—and connected devices are how the sensors spread. In the case of drones, this means they can not only download up-to-date 3-D maps of their world to help them navigate but also potentially *upload* data to make those maps better.

Cool Is Not Enough

Where all this really kicks in is the enterprise. There, nobody is using a drone because it's cool. They're using it because it does a job better than the alternative. All that matters is the job, and every step that stands between wanting the job done and having it done is friction that inhibits adoption. The perfect enterprise drone is a box with a red button. When you push the button, you get your data. Anything more complicated is a pain point to be eliminated. (And after that, we'll get rid of the button, too.)

What that means is seamless integration between drones and enterprise software, such that all the data is automatically collected, sent to the cloud, analyzed, and displayed in useful form, ideally in near-real time.

What will this look like? Although it might surprise you, I hope the future of drones is boring. As the CEO of a drone company, I obviously stand to gain from the rise of drones, but I don't see that happening if we are focused on the *excitement* of drones. The sign of a successful technology is not that it thrills but that it becomes essential and accepted, fading into the wallpaper of modernity. Electricity was once a magic trick, but now it is assumed. The internet is going the same way. My end goal is for drones to be thought of as just another unsexy industrial tool, like agricultural machinery or generators on construction sites—as obviously useful as they are unremarkable.

My inspiration in this is my grandfather, Fred Hauser, who in the 1930s invented the automatic sprinkler system (his patents decorate our walls). You may not think of a sprinkler system as a robot, but it is: Today's are connected to the internet, collect data, operate autonomously, and, best of all, just work. Now imagine farm drones doing the same: boxes scattered around the farm with copters inside and solar cells outside, to recharge their batteries. Like the irrigation systems, at some point in the day they wake up, emerge from the boxes, and do their thing—crop mapping, pest spotting, or even fertilizing like bees. When they're done, they return automatically to their boxes; the lids close, and they sleep until they do it all again the next day. All the farmer needs to know is that the daily crop report on his or her phone is extraordinarily detailed, with multispectral analysis of everything from disease to dampness, measured to the individual leaf and analyzed by machine-learning software to flag issues and make recommendations for the day's work.

Drones as ubiquitous as sprinklers: We've come a long way from weapons, sci-fi movies, and headlines. But in the prosaic applications of advanced technologies lie their real impact. Once we find drones no longer novel enough to be worthy of HBR articles, my work will be done.

Drones Take Off

BY JUST ABOUT ANY METRIC, the drone economy is growing rapidly. This portfolio of charts shows what to expect over the next five years. The big takeaway: The number of drones, pilots, and applications will surge. We're entering the commercial drone era.

Commercial drones are set to take off

Forecasts vary, but anywhere from a quarter-million to a million-and-a-half working drones will enter U.S. skies in the next four years.

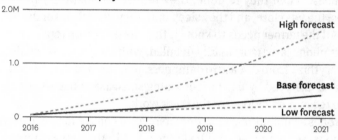

Source: FAA

Money is moving to software

Drone investments are moving away from the hardware and operators and toward the software and services. Autonomous drones will push this trend even further.

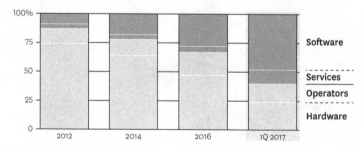

Source: DRONEII.com

88

Pilots needed

In every scenario, the number of remote pilots registered as commercial operators will rise, but the growth will be somewhat slower if the FAA changes regulations to allow a single pilot to operate multiple drones at once. Regulations that allow autonomous flight would further dampen growth but would increase the need for software engineers and drone traffic controllers.

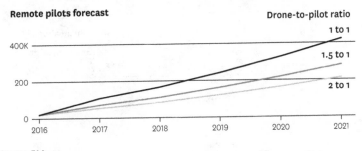

Remote pilots forecast

Drone-to-pilot ratio

Source: FAA

The three waves of the drone economy

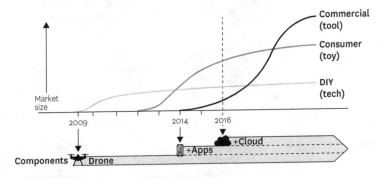

Source: Chris Anderson

Autonomy changes the game

Piloted drones offer major benefits in surveying small areas, but they don't scale. Autonomous drones will revolutionize large-area data collection.

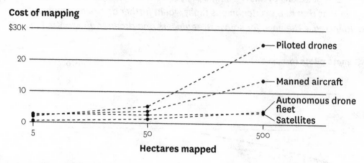

Cost of mapping

Source: Chris Anderson

The right drone for the job

Different drones do different jobs. Make sure you hire the right one.

	Fixed wing	Rotary wing
Cruising speed	High	Low
Coverage area	Large	Small
Object resolution	Centimeter or inch per pixel	Millimeter per pixel
Takeoff/landing area needed	Large	Very small
Flight time and wind resistance	High	Low
Applications	Agriculture Construction Environmental management GIS (mapping) Humanitarian work Rural surveying Mining	Cinematography Construction Emergency response Inspection Law enforcement Real estate Urban surveying

Source: "Drone Industry Report," Oppenheimer & Co., February 2016

What are businesses using drones for right now?

Photography was the first killer app for drones. Surveying and mapping followed. Among the apps not on this list but rapidly gaining users are journalism, TV and film, and communications infrastructure.

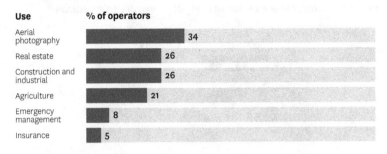

Use   **% of operators**

Use	% of operators
Aerial photography	34
Real estate	26
Construction and industrial	26
Agriculture	21
Emergency management	8
Insurance	5

Source: FAA
Note: Total exceeds 100% because some operators work in multiple industries.

What drone operators want to do that the law prohibits

The top five commercial waiver requests received by the FAA:

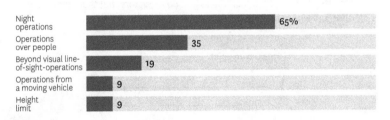

Night operations	65%
Operations over people	35
Beyond visual line-of-sight-operations	19
Operations from a moving vehicle	9
Height limit	9

Source: FAA
Note: Total exceeds 100% because one request can include multiple types of waivers.

Where the savings are

Case study

A 7.5-hectare construction site was surveyed by conventional means and by a drone. The savings were in operations: Two people needed 11.5 hours using conventional means, but one person needed just 50 minutes using a drone.

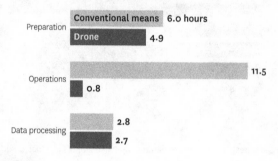

Preparation
Conventional means 6.0 hours
Drone 4.9

Operations
11.5
0.8

Data processing
2.8
2.7

Source: DRONEII.com

Amortization period of inital investment

The initial cost of a single drone mission is higher than that of conventional means, because of acquisition, insurance, and other factors. But that investment pays off after just eight missions.

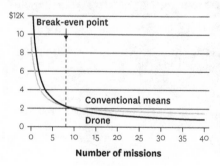

Break-even point

Conventional means

Drone

Number of missions

Technical evolution

As jobs for drones evolve, drone technology changes too. Here's how close various advances are to reality.

Development stage

Early	Mid	Late
Long-lasting batteries and other power sources	Advanced manufacturing techniques	Communication systems
	Obstacle avoidance capabilities	GPS integration
	Advanced engines	Data processing
	Lighter-weight structures	Sensors

Source: "Drone Industry Report," Oppenheimer & Co., February 2016

Jobs for drones

As more industries look at drone technology, the list of jobs drones can do—or could do—is growing. But what's real?

Development stage

Early	Mid	Late
Mail/small package delivery	Construction/real estate images and monitoring	Aerial photography
	Emergency management	Border patrol
	Filmmaking/other media	Precision agriculture
	Infrastructure monitoring	Public safety
	Oil and gas exploration	
	Weather forecasting/meteorological research	
	Wildlife/environmental monitoring	

Source: "Drone Industry Report," Oppenheimer & Co., February 2016

Originally published in May 2017. Reprint BG1703

The Truth About Blockchain

by Marco Iansiti and Karim R. Lakhani

CONTRACTS, TRANSACTIONS, AND THE RECORDS of them are among the defining structures in our economic, legal, and political systems. They protect assets and set organizational boundaries. They establish and verify identities and chronicle events. They govern interactions among nations, organizations, communities, and individuals. They guide managerial and social action. And yet these critical tools and the bureaucracies formed to manage them have not kept up with the economy's digital transformation. They're like a rush-hour gridlock trapping a Formula 1 race car. In a digital world, the way we regulate and maintain administrative control has to change.

Blockchain promises to solve this problem. The technology at the heart of bitcoin and other virtual currencies, blockchain is an open, distributed ledger that can record transactions between two parties efficiently and in a verifiable and permanent way. The ledger itself can also be programmed to trigger transactions automatically. (See the sidebar "How Blockchain Works.")

With blockchain, we can imagine a world in which contracts are embedded in digital code and stored in transparent, shared databases, where they are protected from deletion, tampering, and revision. In this world every agreement, every process, every task, and every payment would have a digital record and signature that could be identified, validated, stored, and shared. Intermediaries

How Blockchain Works

Here are five basic principles underlying the technology.

1. **Distributed database.** Each party on a blockchain has access to the entire database and its complete history. No single party controls the data or the information. Every party can verify the records of its transaction partners directly, without an intermediary.

2. **Peer-to-peer transmission.** Communication occurs directly between peers instead of through a central node. Each node stores and forwards information to all other nodes.

3. **Transparency with pseudonymity.** Every transaction and its associated value are visible to anyone with access to the system. Each node, or user, on a blockchain has a unique 30-plus-character alphanumeric address that identifies it. Users can choose to remain anonymous or provide proof of their identity to others. Transactions occur between blockchain addresses.

4. **Irreversibility of records.** Once a transaction is entered in the database and the accounts are updated, the records cannot be altered, because they're linked to every transaction record that came before them (hence the term "chain"). Various computational algorithms and approaches are deployed to ensure that the recording on the database is permanent, chronologically ordered, and available to all others on the network.

5. **Computational logic.** The digital nature of the ledger means that blockchain transactions can be tied to computational logic and in essence programmed. So users can set up algorithms and rules that automatically trigger transactions between nodes.

like lawyers, brokers, and bankers might no longer be necessary. Individuals, organizations, machines, and algorithms would freely transact and interact with one another with little friction. This is the immense potential of blockchain.

Indeed, virtually everyone has heard the claim that blockchain will revolutionize business and redefine companies and economies. Although we share the enthusiasm for its potential, we worry about the hype. It's not just security issues (such as the 2014 collapse of one bitcoin exchange and the more recent hacks of others) that concern us. Our experience studying technological innovation tells us that if

Idea in Brief

The Hype

We've all heard that blockchain will revolutionize business, but it's going to take a lot longer than many people claim.

The Reason

Like TCP/IP (on which the internet was built), blockchain is a foundational technology that will require broad coordination. The level of complexity—technological, regulatory, and social—will be unprecedented.

The Truth

The adoption of TCP/IP suggests blockchain will follow a fairly predictable path. While the journey will take years, it's not too early for businesses to start planning.

there's to be a blockchain revolution, many barriers—technological, governance, organizational, and even societal—will have to fall. It would be a mistake to rush headlong into blockchain innovation without understanding how it is likely to take hold.

True blockchain-led transformation of business and government, we believe, is still many years away. That's because blockchain is not a "disruptive" technology, which can attack a traditional business model with a lower-cost solution and overtake incumbent firms quickly. Blockchain is a *foundational* technology: It has the potential to create new foundations for our economic and social systems. But while the impact will be enormous, it will take decades for blockchain to seep into our economic and social infrastructure. The process of adoption will be gradual and steady, not sudden, as waves of technological and institutional change gain momentum. That insight and its strategic implications are what we'll explore in this article.

Patterns of Technology Adoption

Before jumping into blockchain strategy and investment, let's reflect on what we know about technology adoption and, in particular, the transformation process typical of other foundational technologies. One of the most relevant examples is distributed computer networking technology, seen in the adoption of TCP/IP (transmission control protocol/internet protocol), which laid the groundwork for the development of the internet.

Introduced in 1972, TCP/IP first gained traction in a *single-use* case: as the basis for e-mail among the researchers on ARPAnet, the U.S. Department of Defense precursor to the commercial internet. Before TCP/IP, telecommunications architecture was based on "circuit switching," in which connections between two parties or machines had to be preestablished and sustained throughout an exchange. To ensure that any two nodes could communicate, telecom service providers and equipment manufacturers had invested billions in building dedicated lines.

TCP/IP turned that model on its head. The new protocol transmitted information by digitizing it and breaking it up into very small packets, each including address information. Once released into the network, the packets could take any route to the recipient. Smart sending and receiving nodes at the network's edges could disassemble and reassemble the packets and interpret the encoded data. There was no need for dedicated private lines or massive infrastructure. TCP/IP created an open, shared public network without any central authority or party responsible for its maintenance and improvement.

Traditional telecommunications and computing sectors looked on TCP/IP with skepticism. Few imagined that robust data, messaging, voice, and video connections could be established on the new architecture or that the associated system could be secure and scale up. But during the late 1980s and 1990s, a growing number of firms, such as Sun, NeXT, Hewlett-Packard, and Silicon Graphics, used TCP/IP, in part to create *localized* private networks within organizations. To do so, they developed building blocks and tools that broadened its use beyond e-mail, gradually replacing more-traditional local network technologies and standards. As organizations adopted these building blocks and tools, they saw dramatic gains in productivity.

TCP/IP burst into broad public use with the advent of the World Wide Web in the mid-1990s. New technology companies quickly emerged to provide the "plumbing"—the hardware, software, and services needed to connect to the now-public network and exchange information. Netscape commercialized browsers, web servers, and other tools and components that aided the development and adoption of internet services and applications. Sun drove the development of Java, the application-programming language. As information on the web grew exponentially, Infoseek, Excite, AltaVista, and Yahoo were born to guide users around it.

Once this basic infrastructure gained critical mass, a new generation of companies took advantage of low-cost connectivity by creating internet services that were compelling *substitutes* for existing businesses. CNET moved news online. Amazon offered more books for sale than any bookshop. Priceline and Expedia made it easier to buy airline tickets and brought unprecedented transparency to the process. The ability of these newcomers to get extensive reach at relatively low cost put significant pressure on traditional businesses like newspapers and brick-and-mortar retailers.

Relying on broad internet connectivity, the next wave of companies created novel, *transformative* applications that fundamentally changed the way businesses created and captured value. These companies were built on a new peer-to-peer architecture and generated value by coordinating distributed networks of users. Think of how eBay changed online retail through auctions, Napster changed the music industry, Skype changed telecommunications, and Google, which exploited user-generated links to provide more relevant results, changed web search.

Ultimately, it took more than 30 years for TCP/IP to move through all the phases—single use, localized use, substitution, and transformation—and reshape the economy. Today more than half the world's most valuable public companies have internet-driven, platform-based business models. The very foundations of our economy have changed. Physical scale and unique intellectual property no longer confer unbeatable advantages; increasingly, the economic leaders are enterprises that act as "keystones," proactively organizing, influencing, and coordinating widespread networks of communities, users, and organizations.

The New Architecture

Blockchain—a peer-to-peer network that sits on top of the internet—was introduced in October 2008 as part of a proposal for bitcoin, a virtual currency system that eschewed a central authority for issuing currency, transferring ownership, and confirming transactions. Bitcoin is the first application of blockchain technology.

The parallels between blockchain and TCP/IP are clear. Just as e-mail enabled bilateral messaging, bitcoin enables bilateral financial transactions. The development and maintenance of blockchain is open, distributed, and shared—just like TCP/IP's. A team of volunteers around the world maintains the core software. And just like e-mail, bitcoin first caught on with an enthusiastic but relatively small community.

TCP/IP unlocked new economic value by dramatically lowering the cost of connections. Similarly, blockchain could dramatically reduce the cost of transactions. It has the potential to become the system of record for all transactions. If that happens, the economy will once again undergo a radical shift, as new, blockchain-based sources of influence and control emerge.

Consider how business works now. Keeping ongoing records of transactions is a core function of any business. Those records track past actions and performance and guide planning for the future. They provide a view not only of how the organization works internally but also of the organization's outside relationships. Every organization keeps its own records, and they're private. Many organizations have no master ledger of all their activities; instead records are distributed across internal units and functions. The problem is, reconciling transactions across individual and private ledgers takes a lot of time and is prone to error.

For example, a typical stock transaction can be executed within microseconds, often without human intervention. However, the settlement—the ownership transfer of the stock—can take as long as a week. That's because the parties have no access to each other's ledgers and can't automatically verify that the assets are in fact owned and can be transferred. Instead a series of intermediaries act as guarantors of assets as the record of the transaction traverses organizations and the ledgers are individually updated.

In a blockchain system, the ledger is replicated in a large number of identical databases, each hosted and maintained by an interested party. When changes are entered in one copy, all the other copies are simultaneously updated. So as transactions occur, records of the value and assets exchanged are permanently entered in all ledgers. There is no need for third-party intermediaries to verify or transfer ownership. If a stock transaction took place on a blockchain-based system, it would be settled within seconds, securely and verifiably. (The infamous hacks that have hit bitcoin exchanges exposed weaknesses not in the blockchain itself but in separate systems linked to parties using the blockchain.)

A Framework for Blockchain Adoption

If bitcoin is like early e-mail, is blockchain decades from reaching its full potential? In our view the answer is a qualified yes. We can't predict exactly how many years the transformation will take, but we can guess which kinds of applications will gain traction first and how blockchain's broad acceptance will eventually come about.

In our analysis, history suggests that two dimensions affect how a foundational technology and its business use cases evolve. The first is novelty—the degree to which an application is new to the world. The more novel it is, the more effort will be required to ensure that users understand what problems it solves. The second dimension is complexity, represented by the level of ecosystem coordination involved—the number and diversity of parties that need to work together to produce value with the technology. For example, a social network with just one member is of little use; a social network is worthwhile only when many of your own connections have signed on to it. Other users of the application must be brought on board to generate value for all participants. The same will be true for many blockchain applications. And, as the scale and impact of those applications increase, their adoption will require significant institutional change.

How foundational technologies take hold

The adoption of foundational technologies typically happens in four phases. Each phase is defined by the novelty of the applications and the complexity of the coordination efforts needed to make them workable. Applications low in novelty and complexity gain acceptance first. Applications high in novelty and complexity take decades to evolve but can transform the economy. TCP/IP technology, introduced on ARPAnet in 1972, has already reached the transformation phase, but blockchain applications (in white) are in their early days.

High

	Substitution	Transformation
Amount of complexity and coordination	Retailer gift cards based on bitcoin Amazon online bookstore	Self-executing smart contracts Skype
	Single use	**Localization**
	Bitcoin payments E-mail on ARPAnet	Private online ledgers for processing financial transactions Internal corporate e-mail networks

Low   Degree of novelty   High

We've developed a framework that maps innovations against these two contextual dimensions, dividing them into quadrants. (See the exhibit "How foundational technologies take hold.") Each quadrant represents a stage of technology development. Identifying which one a blockchain innovation falls into will help executives understand the types of challenges it presents, the level of collaboration and consensus it needs, and the legislative and regulatory efforts it will require. The map will also suggest what kind of processes and infrastructure must be established to facilitate the innovation's adoption. Managers can use it to assess the state of blockchain development in any industry, as well as to evaluate strategic investments in their own blockchain capabilities.

Single use

In the first quadrant are low-novelty and low-coordination applications that create better, less costly, highly focused solutions. E-mail, a cheap alternative to phone calls, faxes, and snail mail, was a single-use application for TCP/IP (even though its value rose with the number of users). Bitcoin, too, falls into this quadrant. Even in its early days, bitcoin offered immediate value to the few people who used it simply as an alternative payment method. (You can think of it as a complex e-mail that transfers not just information but also actual value.) At the end of 2016 the value of bitcoin transactions was expected to hit $92 billion. That's still a rounding error compared with the $411 trillion in total global payments, but bitcoin is growing fast and increasingly important in contexts such as instant payments and foreign currency and asset trading, where the present financial system has limitations.

Localization

The second quadrant comprises innovations that are relatively high in novelty but need only a limited number of users to create immediate value, so it's still relatively easy to promote their adoption. If blockchain follows the path network technologies took in business, we can expect blockchain innovations to build on single-use applications to create local private networks on which multiple organizations are connected through a distributed ledger.

Much of the initial private blockchain-based development is taking place in the financial services sector, often within small networks of firms, so the coordination requirements are relatively modest. Nasdaq is working with Chain.com, one of many blockchain infrastructure providers, to offer technology for processing and validating financial transactions. Bank of America, JPMorgan, the New York Stock Exchange, Fidelity Investments, and Standard Chartered are testing blockchain technology as a replacement for paper-based and manual transaction processing in such areas as trade finance, foreign exchange, cross-border settlement, and securities settlement. The Bank of Canada is testing a digital currency called CAD-coin for interbank transfers. We anticipate a proliferation of private blockchains that serve specific purposes for various industries.

Substitution

The third quadrant contains applications that are relatively low in novelty because they build on existing single-use and localized applications, but are high in coordination needs because they involve broader and increasingly public uses. These innovations aim to replace entire ways of doing business. They face high barriers to adoption, however; not only do they require more coordination but the processes they hope to replace may be full-blown and deeply embedded within organizations and institutions. Examples of substitutes include cryptocurrencies—new, fully formed currency systems that have grown out of the simple bitcoin payment technology. The critical difference is that a cryptocurrency requires every party that does monetary transactions to adopt it, challenging governments and institutions that have long handled and overseen such transactions. Consumers also have to change their behavior and understand how to implement the new functional capability of the cryptocurrency.

A recent experiment at MIT highlights the challenges ahead for digital currency systems. In 2014 the MIT Bitcoin Club provided each of MIT's 4,494 undergraduates with $100 in bitcoin. Interestingly, 30% of the students did not even sign up for the free money, and 20% of the sign-ups converted the bitcoin to cash within a few weeks. Even the technically savvy had a tough time understanding how or where to use bitcoin.

One of the most ambitious substitute blockchain applications is Stellar, a nonprofit that aims to bring affordable financial services, including banking, micropayments, and remittances, to people who've never had access to them. Stellar offers its own virtual currency, lumens, and also allows users to retain on its system a range of assets, including other currencies, telephone minutes, and data credits. Stellar initially focused on Africa, particularly Nigeria, the largest economy there. It has seen significant adoption among its target population and proved its cost-effectiveness. But its future is by no means certain, because the ecosystem coordination challenges are high. Although grassroots adoption has demonstrated the viability of Stellar, to become a banking standard, it will need to influence government policy and persuade central banks and large organizations to use it. That could take years of concerted effort.

Transformation
Into the last quadrant fall completely novel applications that, if successful, could change the very nature of economic, social, and political systems. They involve coordinating the activity of many actors and gaining institutional agreement on standards and processes. Their adoption will require major social, legal, and political change.

"Smart contracts" may be the most transformative blockchain application at the moment. These automate payments and the transfer of currency or other assets as negotiated conditions are met. For example, a smart contract might send a payment to a supplier as soon as a shipment is delivered. A firm could signal via blockchain that a particular good has been received—or the product could have GPS functionality, which would automatically log a location update that, in turn, triggered a payment. We've already seen a few early experiments with such self-executing contracts in the areas of venture funding, banking, and digital rights management.

The implications are fascinating. Firms are built on contracts, from incorporation to buyer-supplier relationships to employee relations. If contracts are automated, then what will happen to traditional firm structures, processes, and intermediaries like lawyers and accountants? And what about managers? Their roles would all radically change. Before we get too excited here, though, let's remember that we are decades away from the widespread adoption of smart contracts. They cannot be effective, for instance, without institutional buy-in. A tremendous degree of coordination and clarity on how smart contracts are designed, verified, implemented, and enforced will be required. We believe the institutions responsible for those daunting tasks will take a long time to evolve. And the technology challenges—especially security—are daunting.

Guiding Your Approach to Blockchain Investment

How should executives think about blockchain for their own organizations? Our framework can help companies identify the right opportunities.

For most, the easiest place to start is single-use applications, which minimize risk because they aren't new and involve little coordination with third parties. One strategy is to add bitcoin as a payment mechanism. The infrastructure and market for bitcoin are already well developed, and adopting the virtual currency will force a variety of functions, including IT, finance, accounting, sales, and marketing, to build blockchain capabilities. Another low-risk approach is to use blockchain internally as a database for applications like managing physical and digital assets, recording internal transactions, and verifying identities. This may be an especially useful solution for companies struggling to reconcile multiple internal databases. Testing out single-use applications will help organizations develop the skills they need for more-advanced applications. And thanks to the emergence of cloud-based blockchain services from both start-ups and large platforms like Amazon and Microsoft, experimentation is getting easier all the time.

Localized applications are a natural next step for companies. We're seeing a lot of investment in private blockchain networks right now, and the projects involved seem poised for real short-term impact. Financial services companies, for example, are finding that the private blockchain networks they've set up with a limited number of trusted counterparties can significantly reduce transaction costs.

Organizations can also tackle specific problems in transactions across boundaries with localized applications. Companies are already using blockchain to track items through complex supply chains, for instance. This is happening in the diamond industry, where gems are being traced from mines to consumers. The technology for such experiments is now available off-the-shelf.

Developing substitute applications requires careful planning, since existing solutions may be difficult to dislodge. One way to go may be to focus on replacements that won't require end users to change their behavior much but present alternatives to expensive or unattractive solutions. To get traction, substitutes must deliver functionality as good as a traditional solution's and must be easy for the ecosystem to absorb and adopt. First Data's foray into blockchain-based gift cards is a good example of a well-considered substitute. Retailers that offer them to consumers can dramatically lower costs per transaction and enhance security by using blockchain to track the flows of currency within accounts—without relying on external payment processors. These new gift cards even allow transfers of balances and transaction capability between merchants via the common ledger.

Transformative applications are still far away. But it makes sense to evaluate their possibilities now and invest in developing technology that can enable them. They will be most powerful when tied to a new business model in which the logic of value creation and capture departs from existing approaches. Such business models are hard to adopt but can unlock future growth for companies.

Consider how law firms will have to change to make smart contracts viable. They'll need to develop new expertise in software and blockchain programming. They'll probably also have to rethink their hourly payment model and entertain the idea of charging transaction or hosting fees for contracts, to name just two possible approaches. Whatever tack they take, executives must be sure they understand and have tested the business model implications before making any switch.

Transformative scenarios will take off last, but they will also deliver enormous value. Two areas where they could have a profound impact: large-scale public identity systems for such functions as passport control, and algorithm-driven decision making in the prevention of money laundering and in complex financial transactions that involve many parties. We expect these applications won't reach broad adoption and critical mass for at least another decade and probably more.

Transformative applications will also give rise to new platform-level players that will coordinate and govern the new ecosystems. These will be the Googles and Facebooks of the next generation. It will require patience to realize such opportunities. Though it may be premature to start making significant investments in them now, developing the required foundations for them—tools and standards—is still worthwhile.

In addition to providing a good template for blockchain's adoption, TCP/IP has most likely smoothed the way for it. TCP/IP has become ubiquitous, and blockchain applications are being built on top of the digital data, communication, and computation infrastructure, which lowers the cost of experimentation and will allow new use cases to emerge rapidly.

With our framework, executives can figure out where to start building their organizational capabilities for blockchain today. They need to ensure that their staffs learn about blockchain, to develop company-specific applications across the quadrants we've identified, and to invest in blockchain infrastructure.

But given the time horizons, barriers to adoption, and sheer complexity involved in getting to TCP/IP levels of acceptance, executives should think carefully about the risks involved in experimenting with blockchain. Clearly, starting small is a good way to develop the know-how to think bigger. But the level of investment should depend on the context of the company and the industry. Financial services companies are already well down the road to blockchain adoption. Manufacturing is not.

No matter what the context, there's a strong possibility that blockchain will affect your business. The very big question is when.

Originally published in January–February 2017. Reprint R1701J

The 3-D Printing Playbook

by Richard A. D'Aveni

A NEW ERA IN ADDITIVE MANUFACTURING, or "3-D printing," is at hand, with major implications for adoption of the technology and for business models that companies can use in taking the plunge. In the three years since I last wrote about the field for HBR ("The 3-D Printing Revolution," May 2015), additive's growing capabilities, together with expansion in both the materials available and the supplier ecosystem, have made it possible to affordably produce a much broader range of things—from the soles of running shoes to turbine blades—often in much higher volumes. The technology provides an unprecedented ability to customize products and respond quickly to shifts in market demand. As a result, it is moving from limited applications, such as prototyping and making conventional machine tools, to a central role in manufacturing for a growing number of industries.

Strategically, that means additive is becoming a full-fledged competitive weapon: It can be used to hold on to market leadership, to dethrone a dominant player, or to diversify by exploiting a printer's capability to make products for different industries. Consequently, leaders need to understand additive's range and potential and the possibilities that will open up in the near future. This article offers a playbook.

Recent Advances

Let's start by examining the breakthroughs propelling additive manufacturing's spread. Technological advances have led to dramatic gains in efficiency and expanded applications in a wide range of areas. The new machines put out products much faster and at lower cost, and the items that emerge from them require less finish work than they did with earlier 3-D printers. Some of these advances are:

- **Faster, more precise printer heads.** Used mainly for plastic products, they can deposit material at 12 to 25 times the speed that was possible three years ago, making them competitive with injection-molding processes for many if not most of those products.

- **Faster powder deposition.** New powder-jetting systems that use binding agents and adhesives can build up complex parts for metal and plastic goods 80 to 100 times as fast as laser-based printers can. These parts cost on average only $4 versus $40 and are made in minutes, not hours.

- **Continuous liquid interface production (CLIP).** Plastic objects are pulled continuously from a vat of resin instead of being built up layer by layer. While not quite as fast or as inexpensive as layer-based additive, CLIP is still economical for mass production, and it offers advantages in finishing, the making of complex parts, and the materials it can use.

- **Electronics-embedding technologies.** New machines can print electronic circuitry and components such as antennae and sensors directly onto the walls of objects. This lessens the need for assembly, frees up space within products, and improves the electronic integration of the entire product, reducing manufacturing waste and enhancing quality. The increasing precision of the machines means that they can be used, for instance, to produce OLED (organic light-emitting diode) display screens.

Idea in Brief

The Advances

Additive manufacturing technology has progressed, and its supplier ecosystem and the materials available have expanded. That means 3-D printing machines can now produce a much wider range of products—affordably and often in greater volume.

The Opportunities

The technology is finally ready to go mainstream: It is competitive

with conventional manufacturing; can produce complex, high-performance structures; and can easily switch from making one item to making another.

The Implications

Companies should consider new business models and strategies to exploit the opportunities and defend themselves against rivals that use 3-D printing.

The benefits of these advances are amplified by breakthroughs in materials. Manufacturers can choose from a much wider range of them, including high-tech alloys for jet-engine parts and other products with demanding performance requirements. Composites, such as very strong plastics infused with glass fiber, carbon fiber, and carbon nanotubes, can replace metals in many cases. Most of these materials are available from multiple sellers, so manufacturers aren't forced to buy proprietary materials from the printer makers at higher prices.

Vast expansion in the additive ecosystem makes it much easier for companies to adopt the new technologies. The ecosystem now includes an array of contract printers, consultants, and suppliers of software and quality-control scanning systems along with makers of printers and materials. Participants range from start-ups to giants such as Siemens, Dassault Systèmes, and DowDuPont. The field has entered a virtuous cycle: A larger ecosystem leads to more applications and lower costs, inducing more manufacturers to adopt the technology, which attracts even more players to the ecosystem.

Additive is fulfilling its promise. It is now competitive with conventional manufacturing in its ability to make tens and even hundreds of thousands of units a year. Factories can use optimizing software to adjust production (changing the number of units or switching between items made) or upgrade products on the fly, at low cost, rather than having to shut down while expanding, retooling, or altering the expensive assembly lines used in conventional plants. Additive also allows companies to make intricate products that can't be made with the subtractive (CNC cutting and drilling) or formative (injection molding) techniques at the heart of conventional manufacturing. And finally, additive is much less capital-intensive than conventional mass-manufacturing equipment: A printer costing less than $1 million can replace a $20 million machine, making it feasible to have many smaller production sites and locate them close to customers.

All this explains why a growing number of diversified, well-established companies—from BMW to Boeing to the Japanese conglomerate Sumitomo—are buying up 3-D printers in quantity, or even printer manufacturers. General Electric, which aims not only to use 3-D printers but to sell them to others, has moved very aggressively into the field: It has acquired three printer makers and has developed software to talk to the machines.

As with any emerging technology, current applications will evolve as learning occurs and may morph into something quite different. Some failures and modifications are inevitable, but the breadth of investment and the multitude of business models now being commercialized demonstrate that players in almost all manufacturing industries should be considering additive.

Emerging Business Models

In light of these developments, where should a mass manufacturer start? The most important decision is the business model. So far six have emerged. The first three exploit additive's superiority in product variation relative to traditional manufacturing; the fourth and fifth maximize its benefits in making complex products; and the sixth takes advantage of efficiencies the technology offers. These models can be used by both B2B and B2C businesses. Some of them are further along in practice than others, but together they show the range of possibilities additive currently provides.

1. Mass Customization

This model takes product variation to the extreme. It entails creating one-off products that are precisely adjusted to the needs or whims of individual buyers—adjustments that can be carried out by simply uploading each customer's digital file into a 3-D printer. Thanks to the efficiency and precision of digital technology, these products cost less than conventionally manufactured items but fit individuals' specifications more exactly.

Mass customization is suitable for any large market in which customers are dissatisfied with standardized, conventionally produced offerings and it's easy to collect customer information. Among the many examples are hearing aids, orthodontic braces, prostheses, sunglasses, car and motorcycle accessories, and Christmas tree decorations. In the case of hearing aids, a laser scan of a patient's ear is automatically converted into a production file, and a printer forms the shell. The electronics are still added separately, but that could soon change, given that it's now possible to print them directly into the shell.

This model can rapidly and significantly affect an entire industry. With hearing aids the shift happened in a year and a half, forcing some manufacturers into bankruptcy.

The main competitive challenge is to reduce the cost of acquiring individual customers' information. Hearing-aid companies first needed a scanning device that audiologists could easily use. In this case, customers were willing to go to an audiologist to be measured. In contrast, buyers of custom orthotics and insoles didn't want to visit an expensive podiatrist to be measured. That's why SOLS Systems, which innovated in this area, couldn't make it on its own; it was acquired in 2017 by another footwear company, Aetrex Worldwide. But the development of smartphone apps that allow people to measure their own feet is overcoming the information-collection obstacle. And HP Inc. has devised a 3-D scanning solution, FitStation, that can be placed in stores. The market is poised to take off.

2. Mass Variety

This model targets customers who have strong and varying preferences but don't need products adjusted to their personal specifications. Manufacturers can skip the process of collecting personal information and offer a wide variety of options at affordable prices. As with mass customization, units are one-offs.

Some jewelry manufacturers, for example, take a few basic designs and make hundreds or even thousands of variations, which they can show online or display in stores. The display versions are hollow and made with faux gold or silver. Instead of maintaining a large and costly inventory of pieces that might not sell, retailers can wait for actual demand. With orders in hand, they can have a contract additive manufacturer such as Shapeways produce the items with solid precious metals, order a desired piece from the designer, or acquire a 3-D printer to make the products in-house.

With mass variety, the main competitive challenge is managing choice. Offering a broad selection will expand the market, but presenting buyers with a huge number of possibilities may overwhelm them. And even with additive, each choice adds some design costs. Manufacturers will have to watch the market carefully or use machine learning to continually sense and respond to what consumers want. They must be ready to develop new designs immediately and purge old ones that aren't selling—an approach that's much easier with additive than with conventional manufacturing.

3. Mass Segmentation

This model greatly limits variety, offering only a few dozen versions of a product to customers whose needs are less variable and easier to predict than with the previous two models. It works well for highly segmented markets, such as components designed specifically for popular B2B products. Each version serves a single segment and differs from the others enough that conventional manufacturers would need costly new machine tools to make all of them. Thus additive companies can make them at a lower cost.

All versions of a product can collectively total hundreds of thousands of units or more. So production is in batches rather than one-off. (Even with additive, uploading files, changing materials, and so on entail small switchover costs.) But because it's still easy to switch printers to other products, a company limits batches to the number it is confident it can sell.

This model is also suitable for seasonal, cyclical, or short-term fad markets, which are tough for traditional manufacturers to serve because they must bet on what consumers will want several months in the future to set up an efficient production line. Additive manufacturers, with their much lower setup time and costs, can commit to production closer to when demand actually occurs, offer more choices, and avoid the risk of being stuck with unwanted goods that must be heavily discounted to sell.

RaceWare Direct, a UK firm that makes accessories for serious cyclists, has adopted the mass segmentation model. It sells a variety of handlebar mounts and other durable, lightweight parts. Each version of its mount for GPS devices, for example, sells only a few hundred or a few thousand units. A conventional manufacturer might need to achieve economies of scale by making just one mount for all such devices.

Daimler has moved toward mass segmentation in stages. It initially used additive to make spare parts for older trucks. After it became proficient with the technology, it started producing specialized parts for some current low-volume truck models. As the number of segments served grows and the number of units sold per segment increases, this process will generate enough parts to become a profitable aspect of the business.

The main competitive challenge here lies in deciding on the size of each segment and the number of segments to serve. Smaller segments will better satisfy some customers but can add design and switchover costs—especially if they require different materials or performance specifications.

4. Mass Modularization

Rather than offering customers different versions of a product, this model involves selling a 3-D-printed body with interchangeable modules for insertion. It applies mainly to electronic devices, which can mean everything from cars to fighter jets and drones. So far this approach has been used only for military hardware and some niche automobiles, but it has significant potential—which Facebook, for one, has realized. It bought Nascent Objects, an additive start-up, to create modular versions of its virtual reality headsets and other hardware.

Here's another application: a smartphone that allows customers to buy a base unit and then snap in modules. The base unit's exoskeleton is printed in customized ergonomic shapes or with flashy designs, and users choose which modules to insert over time as their needs and preferences change or as technology advances, negating the need to buy an entirely new phone. Google gave up on such a phone a few years ago, but Moduware, an Australian company, has developed software to help smartphone manufacturers design the base units. Moduware could profit from making the modules used in products designed with its software.

Traditional manufacturers in a range of areas already offer modular products. But 3-D-printed products have two advantages. First, additive allows customization of the base unit. Second, and more important, that unit can be made in a completely new way, with antennae, wiring, and circuits printed directly onto or into its body. This reduces assembly costs, increases opportunities for miniaturization, and creates space for additional electronic components to be integrated into the product in ways that conventional modular production methods cannot manage.

The main competitive challenge here is deciding what to embed in the base unit and what to place in the modules, which affects pricing and product versatility. Putting more into the base unit makes it easier to give a rival's functionality away free, much as Microsoft did by incorporating the browser into its Windows operating system, undermining Netscape.

5. Mass Complexity

The first four models take advantage of additive's flexibility to make a variety of product versions at low cost. This model exploits its ability to make products with intricate designs that conventional manufacturing can't achieve and to produce unusual shapes and embed sensors and other elements. That ability reduces production costs while improving the product's reliability—as Vita-Mix found when it used the CLIP printer to make a nozzle for its commercial mixers. It's now making tens of thousands of those nozzles.

Boeing is using additive to build supports shaped like a honeycomb for airplane fuselages. The intricate structure of the supports makes these load-bearing parts just as strong as the conventional equivalents but with much less material—thereby significantly reducing weight and fuel consumption. Adidas uses CLIP printers to make strong, supple, lightweight lattice structures for the midsoles of running shoes, which are too complex to be made with conventional technology. It expects to print 100,000 pairs in 2018; 500,000 in 2019; and eventually millions a year. These midsoles will absorb the impact of running better than conventional ones do.

With new design software emerging, additive manufacturing can now restructure materials at the micro level to improve properties such as porosity, strength, durability, elasticity, and rigidity. It can even improve a product's resistance to water, chemicals, and bacteria.

The main challenge here is simply the human imagination. Can product developers escape the conventional mindset to design products that take full advantage of additive's potential? If so, mass complexity may expand far beyond high-performance products. And new software from Autodesk, Dassault, and others means that product developers may not even have to do the thinking. This software allows developers to specify certain attributes and then leave it

Advances that are taking 3-D printing mainstream

Here are just some of the technology improvements that are making additive manufacturing competitive with or even superior to conventional factories in a wide range of applications.

Technology	Description	Advantages	Products
Multijet fusion Commercially available *Leading players* HP Inc., voxeljet, Xaar	Thousands of print heads precisely and quickly lay fusing and detailing agents on plastic powder to build up an object.	12 times as fast and half as expensive as previous plastic additive processes and competitive with injection-molding production for manufacturing up to 110,000 units of an average plastic part	Custom shoe insoles; customized dolls for LookReal; exoskeletons for military and defense drones
Continuous liquid interface production (CLIP) Commercially available *Leading player* Carbon	Objects are pulled from a vat of resin that solidifies when exposed to light; oxygen is used to speed up the process.	25 times as fast as (but not significantly cheaper than) conventional stereolithography, especially for making complex nonlinear shapes	Nozzles for Vita-Mix's commercial mixers; mounts for Oracle servers
Aerosol jetting and nano-particle ink jetting Commercially available *Leading players* Optomec, Nano Dimension	Conductive metal inks, dielectric pastes, and semiconductor material are precisely deposited to print electronic components and chips.	Allows electronic circuits and components to be embedded in the product, saving space and assembly costs	Embedded antennae for mobile phones (LITE-ON); high-efficiency solar cells

Technology	Description	Comparison	Applications
Inkjet screen printing Commercially available **Leading players** Kateeva, JOLED, Tokyo Electron	Specialized nozzles spray soluble inks in a nitrogen chamber to print flexible and large OLED screens.	20% to 40% lower production costs, fewer defects, and higher quality (screens last two or three times as long) compared with conventional manufacturing; almost zero waste	Flexible OLEDs for wearables and mobile displays; LG and Samsung large OLED TV screens
Automated parallel printing Scheduled to become commercially available in mid-2018 **Leading player** Formlabs	A series of printers combined with a robotic arm and a finishing function create ready-to-sell plastic products.	First fully automated, "lights-out" system using additive and automation to reduce labor in unloading and moving products to a separate finishing area	Surgical guides for the health care industry; dental molds and crown and bridge models
Single-pass jetting Scheduled to become commercially available in early 2019 **Leading player** Desktop Metal	The high-speed jetting of metal powder is combined with binding agents in a continuous bidirectional process.	100 times as fast as laser-based metal additive manufacturing and 1/20th as expensive	Water impellers (for pumps); drill bits; gears
Carousel conveyor printing In development **Leading player** BigRep (in partnership with TNO)	A moving platform rapidly rotates the product being printed among numerous printheads and finishing functions.	10 times as fast as stationary printing	Customized footwear; spare parts for automotive and transportation industries (in development)

to the computer to generate a design that will optimize performance and cost, overcoming trade-offs that have stymied human designers. Automobiles, for example, could be made both safer and lighter. Such "generative design" may become the killer app that persuades many companies to jump into additive, lest their rivals offer desirable new products that are simply unachievable with conventional techniques.

6. Mass Standardization

This last model attacks traditional manufacturing's home turf. It proves—contrary to naysayers' dismissal of additive as a niche technology that is useful only for small-scale production—that high-volume standard products can be churned out at a low cost in certain circumstances. The technology is still emerging in this area, but it could become a game changer.

Take video screens. Conventional manufacturing processes for OLED screens waste a lot of expensive light-emitting electrochemical materials. Printers now on the market handle these materials more precisely and thereby produce lower-cost, higher-performance screens. Additive-made OLED screens for cell phones and other handheld devices are everywhere; television manufacturers, interested in joining in, are conducting pilot projects for mass-producing TV screens with these printers.

Mass standardization is possible even for low-tech products. Cosyflex, a 3-D printing system made by Tamicare, produces textiles by spraying various mixtures of polymers and natural fibers onto a moving platform. This fully automated system can produce finished goods at lower cost than conventional production can, even at scale. Tamicare is still commercializing its technology, but the results it has seen to date are promising.

Over time, as 3-D printers grow ever more efficient, they may become competitive for making standardized products even when they don't save on direct costs. That's because traditional manufacturing often involves a lot of indirect and overhead costs: an extended and risky supply chain, expensive capital equipment, the elaborate assembly of parts, and high inventory or transportation costs. Additive reduces all those. What's more, the printers themselves are generally less expensive than conventional machines with tool-and-die elements.

The main competitive challenge here is likely to be how much to specialize 3-D printers for these products. Specialization can help achieve the efficiencies needed for mass standardization, but it may increase risk by restricting companies to certain industries.

Strategic Moves

These six business models are not mutually exclusive—a company might find value in both greater variation and greater complexity. GE's fuel nozzles for jet engines combine mass complexity with mass segmentation. The nozzles are complex combinations of many parts, and each kind of jet engine needs a different shape of nozzle. So GE uses additive to make dozens of versions in medium quantities. Adidas's additive midsoles follow the mass complexity model, but a separate line will use mass customization to satisfy high-level runners or those with special orthopedic challenges. To better understand the preferences of its customers, Adidas is considering moving its manufacturing closer to them and perhaps even locating some of it within retail stores.

Once you've gained capabilities in additive, you can apply it in a variety of competitive situations. Here are some ways it can be used against rivals that rely on conventional production:

Blocking out potential competitors

Suppose your company has a strong market position but is vulnerable to rivals' targeting of specific segments. You could use additive to proactively expand your product line and prevent any openings. Hershey seems to be following this strategy with its recent investment in additive. Although it is the dominant player in the U.S. chocolate industry, it has been losing market share to premium foreign companies that might creep into the mass market. Creating its own conventional product line for fancy Italian or Belgian chocolate would be too costly, because the company couldn't sell enough to cover its expensive equipment. But with additive it can economically make chocolate in a range of recipes by using many small printers, each dedicated to a specific country's style—and thereby prevent the foreign rivals from expanding their toehold. Hershey is also hoping that its new chocolate printers become so easy to use that it can sell them to restaurants, bakeries, and pastry shops—thereby blocking rivals that might try to enter the American market through those channels.

Dethroning the market leader

Suppose your company is struggling to compete with the dominant player in your industry, which offers only a few standard products. Because it has the largest market share, the leader's economies of scale enable it to invest more aggressively than your company can. The only way to compete is to change the game. With additive, your company can cheaply produce variations on the standard product and determine whether customers are interested in them. If you attract enough interest, you can adopt one of the variation-based business models. Even if your offerings aren't cheaper than the leader's, you will gain market share, because customers will be happy to benefit from an offering closer to their tastes or needs. As you add more variety to your offerings, you might draw so many customers away from the market leader that it will have to scale down, and its margins will collapse. Even if the leader sees the danger, it will struggle to respond, because the importance of achieving scale economies by making standard products is entrenched in its mindset.

Coexisting with the market leader

What if you find that customer demand for variety isn't sufficient for your company to seize enough market share to dethrone the leader anytime soon? You might still decide to go with additive and focus on just a few segments—again with a variation-based business model. You might be able to restrict your rival to its current markets by preempting its growth opportunities. If not, your company could still profitably coexist with it by using your product variety and niches to avoid direct competition.

Overcoming rivals that have strong supply or distribution chains

A powerful value chain is hard to beat, but additive can change the game by creating an entirely new supply chain for materials and parts. This is especially true with the mass-complexity business model, which allows your company to create new versions of products with fewer parts and different materials. If you have a supplier with additive capacity, you might consolidate the manufacture of many of your company's low-volume parts with it, because it can easily switch between small batches. A similar logic applies to distribution, because additive allows your company to build smaller factories close to customers. (Some companies even have mobile additive factories—printers in a truck that can quickly move to a customer in need.) Because additive makes your factories and your suppliers' more flexible, it generally works to reduce supply chain complexity.

This dynamic can insulate you against supply and distribution risks, which are rising because of increasing protectionism. If a specific part or material suddenly becomes much more expensive—owing to tariffs, natural disasters, or geopolitical tensions—you can redesign the product to use less of it. Or you can reallocate production to a safer site merely by transferring design files to a different additive facility.

This approach is most effective when your rival is forced to depend on long, geographically and technically complex supply or distribution chains.

Exploring and capturing new markets

One way to change the game is to move to adjacent or completely new markets. When ideas or opportunities appear in either place, you can use additive to develop a new product, test the market, modify the product to improve sales, and gain first-mover advantage quickly and less expensively. Additive makes it easier to take an exploratory approach, because it can yield product shapes and structures beyond those currently imagined. And you can invest the profits from a new market to compete better in your existing market. This approach is risky, but it can be a strong choice for ambitious, entrepreneurial companies.

The Coming of Pan-Industrial Manufacturing

Coupled with a powerful software platform, additive manufacturing enables companies to diversify much more widely. For example, in 2015 GE built a remarkable factory in Pune, India. Previously every GE plant had been dedicated to serving a single division, such as aviation, health care, or power generation. But because Pune relies on 3-D printers, it can make parts for multiple divisions, which allows it to keep its capacity-utilization rate higher than if it were serving just one business. (It has some conventional manufacturing equipment as well, to make parts for which additive isn't yet economical.) If jet sales are booming, Pune devotes much of its production to parts for jet engines. But if that business slows, and demand for renewable power takes off, those production lines start making wind turbines. A conventional plant would find it too expensive and time-consuming to make the switch.

The Pune plant relies mostly on a mass-segmentation business model for its diverse products, but as it moves along the learning curve, it may start to employ mass complexity as well.

Thanks to this plant and to other "brilliant factories" that GE has established or intends to build, the company's diversified businesses will reap substantial benefits. To fully realize them, the divisions will need to collaborate. GE may not be a conventional conglomerate much longer. We need a new name to describe a diversified manufacturer that combines additive with software platforms to achieve operational synergies across the entire company. I suggest "pan-industrial." (See my article "Choosing Scope over Focus" in the *Sloan Management Review,* Summer 2017.)

Pan-industrials won't venture into just any industry: The technical expertise needed, the business model, or the materials available will limit their span. They might focus on consumer durables, metal

The Temptation of Industry 4.0

FOR SEVERAL YEARS THE GERMAN GOVERNMENT and some consulting firms have promoted "Industry 4.0," a broad program for digitizing manufacturing with robots, artificial intelligence, the internet of things, and other technological advances. Encouraging companies to digitize and innovate by adding new technologies is a good thing. But some versions of Industry 4.0 still assume conventional, capital-intensive manufacturing techniques and supply chains. That could be a bad thing, because it consigns additive manufacturing to a largely supporting role of prototyping and providing a few specialized parts. Such an incremental approach to digitization will end up protecting the past and preventing the rethinking necessary to take full advantage of additive's capabilities. Factories with heavy investments in conventional equipment will struggle to customize products, make complex parts, reduce assembly, and adjust production to changing market demand.

Consequently, companies that embrace Industry 4.0 are likely to lose out to nimbler rivals that take full advantage of additive's capabilities. Many Industry 4.0 devotees could end up with fixed costs and operational inflexibilities that sink them in the long term.

parts, or plastic industrial goods. But that will still provide much wider scope than anything Wall Street currently tolerates. As companies learn to exploit the full potential of additive, diversification may even become a strategic imperative, ushering in a new era of competition among giant industrial companies.

Many companies are intrigued by the potential of additive manufacturing but wary of the risks. At most they use it to make prototypes and a few low-volume niche products. Now is the time to take it seriously as an option for large-scale commercial production. Companies should move off the sidelines, get familiar with the new techniques, and explore how they might alter the competitive landscape.

Additive has the potential to shake up not just individual industries but the manufacturing sector as a whole. Eventually a technology that engineers once mocked for its slowness may become a dominant force in the economy.

Originally published in July–August 2018. Reprint R1804H

Collaborative Intelligence: Humans and AI Are Joining Forces

by H. James Wilson and Paul R. Daugherty

ARTIFICIAL INTELLIGENCE IS BECOMING good at many "human" jobs—diagnosing disease, translating languages, providing customer service—and it's improving fast. This is raising reasonable fears that AI will ultimately replace human workers throughout the economy. But that's not the inevitable, or even most likely, outcome. Never before have digital tools been so responsive to us, nor we to our tools. While AI will radically alter how work gets done and who does it, the technology's larger impact will be in complementing and augmenting human capabilities, not replacing them.

Certainly, many companies have used AI to automate processes, but those that deploy it mainly to displace employees will see only short-term productivity gains. In our research involving 1,500 companies, we found that firms achieve the most significant performance improvements when humans and machines work together (see the exhibit "The value of collaboration"). Through such collaborative intelligence, humans and AI actively enhance each other's complementary strengths: the leadership, teamwork, creativity, and social skills of the former, and the speed, scalability,

The value of collaboration

Companies benefit from optimizing collaboration between humans and artificial intelligence. Five principles can help them do so: Reimagine business processes; embrace experimentation/employee involvement; actively direct AI strategy; responsibly collect data; and redesign work to incorporate AI and cultivate related employee skills. A survey of 1,075 companies in 12 industries found that the more of these principles companies adopted, the better their AI initiatives performed in terms of speed, cost savings, revenues, or other operational measures.

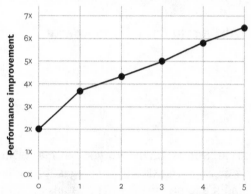

Number of human-machine collaboration principles adopted
(0 indicates the adoption of only basic, noncollaborative AI)

and quantitative capabilities of the latter. What comes naturally to people (making a joke, for example) can be tricky for machines, and what's straightforward for machines (analyzing gigabytes of data) remains virtually impossible for humans. Business requires both kinds of capabilities.

To take full advantage of this collaboration, companies must understand how humans can most effectively augment machines, how machines can enhance what humans do best, and how to redesign business processes to support the partnership. Through our research and work in the field, we have developed guidelines to help companies achieve this and put the power of collaborative intelligence to work.

Idea in Brief

The Outlook

Artificial intelligence is transforming business—and having the most significant impact when it augments human workers instead of replacing them.

The Details

Companies see the biggest performance gains when humans and smart machines collaborate. People are needed to train machines, explain their outputs, and ensure their responsible use. AI, in turn, can enhance humans' cognitive skills and creativity, free workers from low-level tasks, and extend their physical capabilities.

The Prescription

Companies should reimagine their business processes, focusing on using AI to achieve more operational flexibility or speed, greater scale, better decision making, or increased personalization of products and services.

Humans Assisting Machines

Humans need to perform three crucial roles. They must *train* machines to perform certain tasks; *explain* the outcomes of those tasks, especially when the results are counterintuitive or controversial; and *sustain* the responsible use of machines (by, for example, preventing robots from harming humans).

Training

Machine-learning algorithms must be taught how to perform the work they're designed to do. In that effort, huge training data sets are amassed to teach machine-translation apps to handle idiomatic expressions, medical apps to detect disease, and recommendation engines to support financial decision making. In addition, AI systems must be trained how best to interact with humans. While organizations across sectors are now in the early stages of filling trainer roles, leading tech companies and research groups already have mature training staffs and expertise.

Consider Microsoft's AI assistant, Cortana. The bot required extensive training to develop just the right personality: confident, caring, and helpful but not bossy. Instilling those qualities took countless hours of attention by a team that included a poet, a novelist, and a playwright. Similarly, human trainers were needed to develop the personalities of Apple's Siri and Amazon's Alexa to ensure that they accurately reflected their companies' brands. Siri, for example, has just a touch of sassiness, as consumers might expect from Apple.

AI assistants are now being trained to display even more complex and subtle human traits, such as sympathy. The start-up Koko, an offshoot of the MIT Media Lab, has developed technology that can help AI assistants seem to commiserate. For instance, if a user is having a bad day, the Koko system doesn't reply with a canned response such as "I'm sorry to hear that." Instead it may ask for more information and then offer advice to help the person see his issues in a different light. If he were feeling stressed, for instance, Koko might recommend thinking of that tension as a positive emotion that could be channeled into action.

Explaining

As AIs increasingly reach conclusions through processes that are opaque (the so-called black-box problem), they require human experts in the field to explain their behavior to nonexpert users. These "explainers" are particularly important in evidence-based industries, such as law and medicine, where a practitioner needs to understand how an AI weighed inputs into, say, a sentencing or medical recommendation. Explainers are similarly important in helping insurers and law enforcement understand why an autonomous car took actions that led to an accident—or failed to avoid one. And explainers are becoming integral in regulated industries— indeed, in any consumer-facing industry where a machine's output could be challenged as unfair, illegal, or just plain wrong. For instance, the European Union's new General Data Protection Regulation (GDPR) gives consumers the right to receive an explanation for any algorithm-based decision, such as the rate offer on a credit card or mortgage. This is one area where AI will contribute to *increased* employment: Experts estimate that companies will have to create about 75,000 new jobs to administer the GDPR requirements.

Sustaining

In addition to having people who can explain AI outcomes, companies need "sustainers"—employees who continually work to ensure that AI systems are functioning properly, safely, and responsibly.

For example, an array of experts sometimes referred to as safety engineers focus on anticipating and trying to prevent harm by AIs. The developers of industrial robots that work alongside people have paid careful attention to ensuring that they recognize humans nearby and don't endanger them. These experts may also review analysis from explainers when AIs do cause harm, as when a self-driving car is involved in a fatal accident.

Other groups of sustainers make sure that AI systems uphold ethical norms. If an AI system for credit approval, for example, is found to be discriminating against people in certain groups (as has happened), these ethics managers are responsible for investigating and addressing the problem. Playing a similar role, data compliance officers try to ensure that the data that is feeding AI systems complies with the GDPR and other consumer-protection regulations. A related data-use role involves ensuring that AIs manage information responsibly. Like many tech companies, Apple uses AI to collect personal details about from users as they engage with the company's devices and software. The aim is to improve the user experience, but unconstrained data gathering can compromise privacy, anger customers, and run afoul of the law. The company's "differential privacy team" works to make sure that while the AI seeks to learn as much as possible about a group of users in a statistical sense, it is protecting the privacy of individual users.

Machines Assisting Humans

Smart machines are helping humans expand their abilities in three ways. They can *amplify* our cognitive strengths; *interact* with customers and employees to free us for higher-level tasks; and *embody* human skills to extend our physical capabilities.

Enhancing performance

At organizations in all kinds of industries, humans and AI are collaborating to improve five elements of business processes.

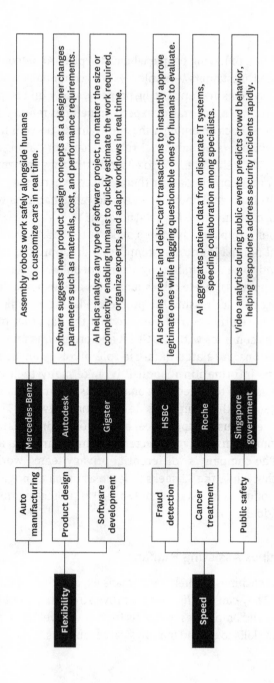

Flexibility

Auto manufacturing	Mercedes-Benz	Assembly robots work safely alongside humans to customize cars in real time.
Product design	Autodesk	Software suggests new product design concepts as a designer changes parameters such as materials, cost, and performance requirements.
Software development	Gigster	AI helps analyze any type of software project, no matter the size or complexity, enabling humans to quickly estimate the work required, organize experts, and adapt workflows in real time.

Speed

Fraud detection	HSBC	AI screens credit- and debit-card transactions to instantly approve legitimate ones while flagging questionable ones for humans to evaluate.
Cancer treatment	Roche	AI aggregates patient data from disparate IT systems, speeding collaboration among specialists.
Public safety	Singapore government	Video analytics during public events predicts crowd behavior, helping responders address security incidents rapidly.

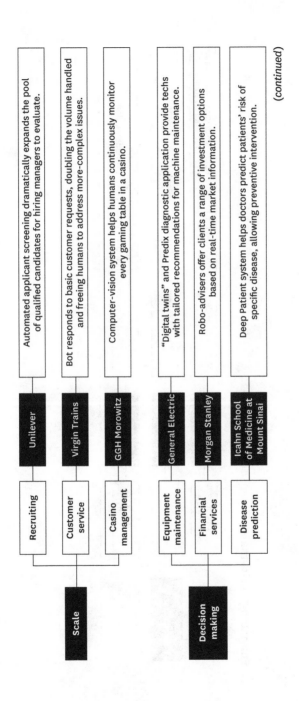

Scale		
Recruiting	Unilever	Automated applicant screening dramatically expands the pool of qualified candidates for hiring managers to evaluate.
Customer service	Virgin Trains	Bot responds to basic customer requests, doubling the volume handled and freeing humans to address more-complex issues.
Casino management	GGH Morowitz	Computer-vision system helps humans continuously monitor every gaming table in a casino.

Decision making		
Equipment maintenance	General Electric	"Digital twins" and Predix diagnostic application provide techs with tailored recommendations for machine maintenance.
Financial services	Morgan Stanley	Robo-advisers offer clients a range of investment options based on real-time market information.
Disease prediction	Icahn School of Medicine at Mount Sinai	Deep Patient system helps doctors predict patients' risk of specific disease, allowing preventive intervention.

(continued)

Enhancing performance (continued)

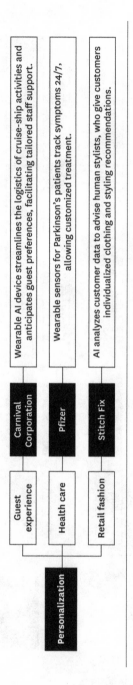

Personalization	Guest experience → Carnival Corporation	Wearable AI device streamlines the logistics of cruise-ship activities and anticipates guest preferences, facilitating tailored staff support.
	Health care → Pfizer	Wearable sensors for Parkinson's patients track symptoms 24/7, allowing customized treatment.
	Retail fashion → Stitch Fix	AI analyzes customer data to advise human stylists, who give customers individualized clothing and styling recommendations.

Amplifying

Artificial intelligence can boost our analytic and decision-making abilities by providing the right information at the right time. But it can also heighten creativity. Consider how Autodesk's Dream-catcher AI enhances the imagination of even exceptional designers. A designer provides Dreamcatcher with criteria about the desired product—for example, a chair able to support up to 300 pounds, with a seat 18 inches off the ground, made of materials costing less than $75, and so on. She can also supply information about other chairs that she finds attractive. Dreamcatcher then churns out thousands of designs that match those criteria, often sparking ideas that the designer might not have initially considered. She can then guide the software, telling it which chairs she likes or doesn't, leading to a new round of designs.

Throughout the iterative process, Dreamcatcher performs the myriad calculations needed to ensure that each proposed design meets the specified criteria. This frees the designer to concentrate on deploying uniquely human strengths: professional judgment and aesthetic sensibilities.

Interacting

Human-machine collaboration enables companies to interact with employees and customers in novel, more effective ways. AI agents like Cortana, for example, can facilitate communications between people or on behalf of people, such as by transcribing a meeting and distributing a voice-searchable version to those who couldn't attend. Such applications are inherently scalable—a single chatbot, for instance, can provide routine customer service to large numbers of people simultaneously, wherever they may be.

SEB, a major Swedish bank, now uses a virtual assistant called Aida to interact with millions of customers. Able to handle natural-language conversations, Aida has access to vast stores of data and can answer many frequently asked questions, such as how to open an account or make cross-border payments. She can also ask callers follow-up questions to solve their problems, and she's able to analyze a caller's tone of voice (frustrated versus appreciative, for instance) and use that information to provide better service later. Whenever the system can't resolve an issue—which happens in about 30% of cases—it turns the caller over to a human customer-service representative and then monitors that interaction to learn how to resolve similar problems in the future. With Aida handling basic requests, human reps can concentrate on addressing more-complex issues, especially those from unhappy callers who might require extra hand-holding.

Embodying

Many AIs, like Aida and Cortana, exist principally as digital entities, but in other applications the intelligence is embodied in a robot that augments a human worker. With their sophisticated sensors, motors, and actuators, AI-enabled machines can now recognize people and objects and work safely alongside humans in factories, warehouses, and laboratories.

In manufacturing, for example, robots are evolving from potentially dangerous and "dumb" industrial machines into smart, context-aware "cobots." A cobot arm might, for example, handle repetitive actions that require heavy lifting, while a person performs complementary tasks that require dexterity and human judgment, such as assembling a gear motor.

Hyundai is extending the cobot concept with exoskeletons. These wearable robotic devices, which adapt to the user and location in real time, will enable industrial workers to perform their jobs with superhuman endurance and strength.

Reimagining Your Business

In order to get the most value from AI, operations need to be redesigned. To do this, companies must first discover and describe an operational area that can be improved. It might be a balky internal process (such as HR's slowness to fill staff positions), or it could be a previously intractable problem that can now be addressed using AI (such as quickly identifying adverse drug reactions across patient

Revealing Invisible Problems

FORMER U.S. DEFENSE SECRETARY Donald Rumsfeld once famously distinguished among "known knowns," "known unknowns," and "unknown unknowns"—things you're not even aware you don't know. Some companies are now using AI to uncover unknown unknowns in their businesses. Case in point: GNS Healthcare applies machine-learning software to find overlooked relationships among data in patients' health records and elsewhere. After identifying a relationship, the software churns out numerous hypotheses to explain it and then suggests which of those are the most likely. This approach enabled GNS to uncover a new drug interaction hidden in unstructured patient notes. CEO Colin Hill points out that this is not garden-variety data mining to find associations. "Our machine-learning platform is not just about seeing patterns and correlations in data," he says. "It's about actually discovering causal links."

populations). Moreover, a number of new AI and advanced analytic techniques can help surface previously invisible problems that are amenable to AI solutions (see the sidebar "Revealing Invisible Problems").

Next, companies must develop a solution through co-creation—having stakeholders envision how they might collaborate with AI systems to improve a process. Consider the case of a large agricultural company that wanted to deploy AI technology to help farmers. An enormous amount of data was available about soil properties, weather patterns, historical harvests, and so forth, and the initial plan was to build an AI application that would more accurately predict future crop yields. But in discussions with farmers, the company learned of a more pressing need. What farmers really wanted was a system that could provide real-time recommendations on how to increase productivity—which crops to plant, where to grow them, how much nitrogen to use in the soil, and so on. The company developed an AI system to provide such advice, and the initial outcomes were promising; farmers were happy about the crop yields obtained with the AI's guidance. Results from that initial test were then fed back into the system to refine the algorithms used. As with the discovery step, new AI and analytic techniques can assist in co-creation by suggesting novel approaches to improving processes.

The third step for companies is to scale and then sustain the proposed solution. SEB, for example, originally deployed a version of Aida internally to assist 15,000 bank employees but thereafter rolled out the chatbot to its one million customers.

Through our work with hundreds of companies, we have identified five characteristics of business processes that companies typically want to improve: flexibility, speed, scale, decision making, and personalization. When reimagining a business process, determine which of these characteristics is central to the desired transformation, how intelligent collaboration could be harnessed to address it, and what alignments and trade-offs with other process characteristics will be necessary.

Flexibility

For Mercedes-Benz executives, inflexible processes presented a growing challenge. Increasingly, the company's most profitable customers had been demanding individualized S-class sedans, but the automaker's assembly systems couldn't deliver the customization people wanted.

Traditionally, car manufacturing has been a rigid process with automated steps executed by "dumb" robots. To improve flexibility, Mercedes replaced some of those robots with AI-enabled cobots and redesigned its processes around human-machine collaborations. At the company's plant near Stuttgart, Germany, cobot arms guided by human workers pick up and place heavy parts, becoming an extension of the worker's body. This system puts the worker in control of the build of each car, doing less manual labor and more of a "piloting" job with the robot.

The company's human-machine teams can adapt on the fly. In the plant, the cobots can be reprogrammed easily with a tablet, allowing them to handle different tasks depending on changes in the workflow. Such agility has enabled the manufacturer to achieve unprecedented levels of customization. Mercedes can individualize vehicle production according to the real-time choices consumers make at dealerships, changing everything from a vehicle's dashboard components to the seat leather to the tire valve caps. As a result, no two cars rolling off the assembly line at the Stuttgart plant are the same.

Speed

For some business activities, the premium is on speed. One such operation is the detection of credit-card fraud. Companies have just seconds to determine whether they should approve a given transaction. If it's fraudulent, they will most likely have to eat that loss. But if they deny a legitimate transaction, they lose the fee from that purchase and anger the customer.

Like most major banks, HSBC has developed an AI-based solution that improves the speed and accuracy of fraud detection. The AI monitors and scores millions of transactions daily, using data on purchase location and customer behavior, IP addresses, and other information to identify subtle patterns that signal possible fraud. HSBC first implemented the system in the United States, significantly reducing the rate of undetected fraud and false positives, and then rolled it out in the UK and Asia. A different AI system used by Danske Bank improved its fraud-detection rate by 50% and decreased false positives by 60%. The reduction in the number of false positives frees investigators to concentrate their efforts on equivocal transactions the AI has flagged, where human judgment is needed.

The fight against financial fraud is like an arms race: Better detection leads to more-devious criminals, which leads to better detection, which continues the cycle. Thus the algorithms and scoring models for combating fraud have a very short shelf life and require continual updating. In addition, different countries and regions use different models. For these reasons, legions of data analysts, IT professionals, and experts in financial fraud are needed at the interface between humans and machines to keep the software a step ahead of the criminals.

Scale

For many business processes, poor scalability is the primary obstacle to improvement. That's particularly true of processes that depend on intensive human labor with minimal machine assistance.

Consider, for instance, the employee recruitment process at Unilever. The consumer goods giant was looking for a way to diversify its 170,000-person workforce. HR determined that it needed to focus on entry-level hires and then fast-track the best into management. But the company's existing processes weren't able to evaluate potential recruits in sufficient numbers—while giving each applicant individual attention—to ensure a diverse population of exceptional talent.

Here's how Unilever combined human and AI capabilities to scale individualized hiring: In the first round of the application process, candidates are asked to play online games that help assess traits such as risk aversion. These games have no right or wrong answers, but they help Unilever's AI figure out which individuals might be best suited for a particular position. In the next round, applicants are asked to submit a video in which they answer questions designed for the specific position they're interested in. Their responses are analyzed by an AI system that considers not just what they say but also their body language and tone. The best candidates from that round, as judged by the AI, are then invited to Unilever for in-person interviews, after which humans make the final hiring decisions.

It's too early to tell whether the new recruiting process has resulted in better employees. The company has been closely tracking the success of those hires, but more data is still needed. It is clear, however, that the new system has greatly broadened the scale of Unilever's recruiting. In part because job seekers can easily access the system by smartphone, the number of applicants doubled to 30,000 within a year, the number of universities represented surged from 840 to 2,600, and the socioeconomic diversity of new hires increased. Furthermore, the average time from application to hiring decision has dropped from four months to just four weeks, while the time that recruiters spend reviewing applications has fallen by 75%.

Decision making

By providing employees with tailored information and guidance, AI can help them reach better decisions. This can be especially valuable for workers in the trenches, where making the right call can have a huge impact on the bottom line.

Consider the way in which equipment maintenance is being improved with the use of "digital twins"—virtual models of physical equipment. General Electric builds such software models of its turbines and other industrial products and continually updates them with operating data streaming from the equipment. By collecting readings from large numbers of machines in the field, GE has amassed a wealth of information on normal and aberrant performance. Its Predix application, which uses machine-learning algorithms, can now predict when a specific part in an individual machine might fail.

This technology has fundamentally changed the decision-intensive process of maintaining industrial equipment. Predix might, for example, identify some unexpected rotor wear and tear in a turbine, check the turbine's operational history, report that the damage has increased fourfold over the past few months, and warn that if nothing is done, the rotor will lose an estimated 70% of its useful life. The system can then suggest appropriate actions, taking into account the machine's current condition, the operating environment, and aggregated data about similar damage and repairs to other machines. Along with its recommendations, Predix can generate information about their costs and financial benefits and provide a confidence level (say, 95%) for the assumptions used in its analysis.

Without Predix, workers would be lucky to catch the rotor damage on a routine maintenance check. It's possible that it would go undetected until the rotor failed, resulting in a costly shutdown. With Predix, maintenance workers are alerted to potential problems before they become serious, and they have the needed information at their fingertips to make good decisions—ones that can sometimes save GE millions of dollars.

Personalization
Providing customers with individually tailored brand experiences is the holy grail of marketing. With AI, such personalization can now be achieved with previously unimaginable precision and at vast scale. Think of the way the music streaming service Pandora uses AI algorithms to generate personalized playlists for each of its millions

of users according to their preferences in songs, artists, and genres. Or consider Starbucks, which, with customers' permission, uses AI to recognize their mobile devices and call up their ordering history to help baristas make serving recommendations. The AI technology does what it does best, sifting through and processing copious amounts of data to recommend certain offerings or actions, and humans do what they do best, exercising their intuition and judgment to make a recommendation or select the best fit from a set of choices.

The Carnival Corporation is applying AI to personalize the cruise experience for millions of vacationers through a wearable device called the Ocean Medallion and a network that allows smart devices to connect. Machine learning dynamically processes the data flowing from the medallion and from sensors and systems throughout the ship to help guests get the most out of their vacations. The medallion streamlines the boarding and debarking processes, tracks the guests' activities, simplifies purchasing by connecting their credit cards to the device, and acts as a room key. It also connects to a system that anticipates guests' preferences, helping crew members deliver personalized service to each guest by suggesting tailored itineraries of activities and dining experiences.

The Need for New Roles and Talent

Reimagining a business process involves more than the implementation of AI technology; it also requires a significant commitment to developing employees with what we call "fusion skills"—those that enable them to work effectively at the human-machine interface. To start, people must learn to delegate tasks to the new technology, as when physicians trust computers to help read X-rays and MRIs. Employees should also know how to combine their distinctive human skills with those of a smart machine to get a better outcome than either could achieve alone, as in robot-assisted surgery. Workers must be able to teach intelligent agents new skills and undergo training to work well within AI-enhanced processes. For example, they must know how best to put questions to an AI agent to get the information they need. And there must be employees, like those on Apple's differential privacy team, who ensure that their companies' AI systems are used responsibly and not for illegal or unethical purposes.

We expect that in the future, company roles will be redesigned around the desired outcomes of reimagined processes, and corporations will increasingly be organized around different types of skills rather than around rigid job titles. AT&T has already begun that transition as it shifts from landline telephone services to mobile networks and starts to retrain 100,000 employees for new positions. As part of that effort, the company has completely overhauled its organizational chart: Approximately 2,000 job titles have been streamlined into a much smaller number of broad categories encompassing similar skills. Some of those skills are what one might expect (for example, proficiency in data science and data wrangling), while others are less obvious (for instance, the ability to use simple machine-learning tools to cross-sell services).

Most activities at the human-machine interface require people to *do new and different things* (such as train a chatbot) and to *do things differently* (use that chatbot to provide better customer service). So far, however, only a small number of the companies we've surveyed have begun to reimagine their business processes to optimize collaborative intelligence. But the lesson is clear: Organizations that use machines merely to displace workers through automation will miss the full potential of AI. Such a strategy is misguided from the get-go. Tomorrow's leaders will instead be those that embrace collaborative intelligence, transforming their operations, their markets, their industries, and—no less important—their workforces.

Originally published in July–August 2018. Reprint R1804J

When Your Boss Wears Metal Pants

by Walter Frick

AT A 2013 ROBOTICS conference the MIT researcher Kate Darling invited attendees to play with animatronic toy dinosaurs called Pleos, which are about the size of a Chihuahua. The participants were told to name their robots and interact with them. They quickly learned that their Pleos could communicate: The dinos made it clear through gestures and facial expressions that they liked to be petted and didn't like to be picked up by the tail. After an hour, Darling gave the participants a break. When they returned, she handed out knives and hatchets and asked them to torture and dismember their Pleos.

Darling was ready for a bit of resistance, but she was surprised by the group's uniform refusal to harm the robots. Some participants went as far as shielding the Pleos with their bodies so that no one could hurt them. "We respond to social cues from these lifelike machines," she concluded in a 2013 lecture, "even if we know that they're not real."

This insight will shape the next wave of automation. As Erik Brynjolfsson and Andrew McAfee describe in their book *The Second Machine Age,* "thinking machines"—from autonomous robots that can quickly learn new tasks on the manufacturing floor to software that can evaluate job applicants or recommend a corporate strategy—are coming to the workplace and may create enormous value for businesses and society. But although technological constraints are dissolving, social ones remain. How can you persuade your team to trust artificial intelligence? Or to accept a robot as a member—or even as a manager? If you replace that robot, will morale suffer?

Answering these questions requires an understanding of how humans will work with and relate to thinking machines. A growing body of research is expanding our knowledge, providing essential insights into how such collaborations can get work done. As these machines evolve from tools to teammates, one thing is clear: Accepting them will be more than a matter of simply adopting new technology.

When We Don't Trust Algorithms—and When We Do

The first challenge in working with thinking machines is recognizing that they often know more than we do. Consider this 2014 finding: Researchers from Wharton ran a series of experiments in which participants were financially rewarded for good predictions and could either go with their own judgment or defer to an algorithm to make those predictions. For example, in one experiment they were shown admissions data for a group of past MBA students and asked to estimate how well each student had performed during the program. Most people preferred to go with their gut rather than defer to the algorithm's estimates.

This phenomenon is called "algorithm avoidance," and it has been documented in many other studies. Whether they're diagnosing patients or forecasting political outcomes, people consistently prefer human judgment—their own or someone else's—to algorithms, and as a result they often make worse decisions. The message for managers is that helping humans to trust thinking machines will be essential.

Unfortunately, simply showing people how well an algorithm performs doesn't make them trust it. When the Wharton researchers let participants see their guesses, the algorithm's, and the correct answers, the participants recognized that the algorithm usually

Idea in Brief

As machines evolve from tools to teammates, the author writes, accepting them will be more than a matter of simply adopting some new technology.

The first challenge will be recognizing when computers know more than we do. "Algorithm avoidance," for instance, makes people prefer human judgment over that of machines and can lead to worse decisions, from diagnosing patients to predicting political outcomes. The message for managers is that helping humans to trust thinking machines will be essential.

One way to encourage that trust is to make robots more humanoid.

Researchers at Carnegie Mellon explored this idea with an autonomous robot named Snackbot, which had wheels, arms, a male voice, and an LED mouth that could smile and frown. People in the office made conversation with it and treated it with kindness. But this approach may lead us to put too much faith in the machines' abilities.

How we work with thinking machines will vary according to the work we're doing, how it's framed, and how the machines are designed. But under the right conditions, people are surprisingly open to a robotic colleague.

performed better. But seeing the results also meant seeing the algorithm's errors, which affected trust. "People lose confidence in algorithms after they've seen them err," says Berkeley Dietvorst, one of the researchers. Even though the humans were wrong more often than the algorithm was, he says, "people don't lose confidence in themselves." In other words, we seem to hold mistakes against an algorithm more than we would against a human being. According to Dietvorst, that's because we believe that human judgment can improve, but we think (falsely) that an algorithm can't.

Algorithm avoidance may be even more pronounced for work that we perceive as more sophisticated or instinctive than number crunching. Researchers from Northwestern's Kellogg School and Harvard Business School asked workers on the crowdsourcing site Mechanical Turk to complete a variety of tasks; some were told that the tasks required "cognition" and "analytical reasoning," while others were told that they required "feeling" and "emotion processing." Then the participants were asked whether they would be comfortable if this sort of work was outsourced to machines. Those who had been told that the work was emotional were far more disturbed by the suggestion than those who had been told it was analytical. "Thinking is almost like doing math," concludes Michael Norton, of HBS, one of the study's authors. "And it's OK for robots to do math. But it's not OK for robots to feel things, because then they're too close to being human."

Norton believes that simply framing a task as analytical could help overcome people's skepticism about algorithms. In another experiment, he and Adam Waytz, of Kellogg, found that people were more likely to be comfortable with the idea of a robot's taking the job of math teacher when they were told that it "requires a lot of analytic skill to teach the students various formulas and algorithms," and less likely to approve when told that it requires "the ability to relate to young people."

Dietvorst and his Wharton colleagues offer another answer. If people prefer their own judgment to an algorithm's, why not incorporate the former into the latter? In one experiment they let people tweak the output of an algorithm slightly. They asked the participants to estimate, on the basis of a variety of data points, how well a high school student had performed on a standardized math test. Rather than being forced to choose between their own estimate and the algorithm's, participants could adjust the algorithm's estimate up or down by a few percentage points and submit the result as their prediction. The researchers found that people given this option were more likely to trust the algorithm. Dietvorst thinks that's because they no longer felt they were giving up control over the forecast.

We Trust Robots More When They Look Like Us

Another way to encourage people to trust thinking machines is to make the latter more humanoid. Studies suggest that giving a machine or an algorithm a voice or a recognizably human body makes it more relatable. Researchers at Northwestern, the University of Connecticut, and the University of Chicago examined this thesis in the context of self-driving cars. In their experiment, participants used a driving simulator and could either do the steering themselves or engage the self-driving feature. In some cases the self-driving feature merely took control of the simulator's steering and speed. In other cases it also had humanoid characteristics—it was named Iris, had a female voice, and spoke to the drivers during the trip. Drivers in Iris-equipped cars were more likely to engage the self-driving feature. The researchers also programmed a simulated accident that appeared to be the fault of another car rather than of the self-driving feature. Participants who experienced the accident with Iris at the wheel were more relaxed and less likely to blame the self-driving feature for causing it than those whose feature had no name or voice.

People trusted Iris more, according to the researchers, because of a tendency toward anthropomorphism—the attribution of human characteristics and motivations, such as the capacity to think, feel, or express intent, to nonhumans. A long line of research suggests that giving machines a voice, a body, or even a name can tap into this tendency and make people more comfortable working with them. For instance, we seem to collaborate with robots more effectively when they make "eye contact" with us, and we think they're cuter and more humanoid when they tilt their heads to one side. (Remember the Pleo?)

Researchers at Carnegie Mellon explored this idea with a four-and-a-half-foot-tall autonomous robot named Snackbot, which had wheels, arms, a male voice, and an LED mouth that could smile and frown. Snackbot's job was to deliver snacks within an office, but it was explicitly designed to evoke an anthropomorphic response. As predicted, people in the office made conversation with it and treated it with kindness. Asked about their interactions with the robot, one participant said, "Snackbot doesn't have feelings, but I wouldn't want to just take the snack and shut the door in its face."

Snackbot was programmed to have "personalized" conversations with some people, commenting on their favorite snacks, for example. Workers who got this treatment were more satisfied with the robot's service and more likely to cooperate when Snackbot made requests of them, such as asking which parts of the office it should add to a tour it would be giving.

But Robots Can Sometimes Be Too Human

One challenge with adding humanoid features to thinking machines is that it may lead us to put too much faith in their abilities. Researchers at the University of Manitoba conducted a series of experiments in which people were asked to do dull, repetitive work: renaming files on a computer. The participants were not told how long the experiment would run—simply that they could leave at any time—but the number of files to be renamed appeared limitless. When, inevitably, they did try to quit, they were prodded to keep going by a two-foot-tall humanoid robot named Jim. Jim sat on a desk, spoke with a robotic voice, gazed inquisitively around the room, and made hand gestures. These features were designed to project intelligence. (Unbeknownst to participants, the robot was actually controlled by researchers and could do little on its own.) When someone tried to quit the task, Jim would say something like "Please continue—we need more data," or "It's essential that you continue." This went on until either the participants ignored the prodding and gave up or 80 minutes had passed. What most struck James Young, one of the study's authors, was that many people "treated the robot as someone they could negotiate with." They argued about how unreasonable it was being by telling them to press on, even though the robot did nothing but repeat the same few phrases. The fact that the robot had a voice and a body seemed to be enough to persuade some people that it had the ability to reason.

Another problem is that as machines become more humanoid, we are likelier to stereotype or even discriminate against them, much as we do with people. An experiment by researchers at Soongsil University, in South Korea, gauged people's satisfaction with a security robot that monitored CCTV footage looking for suspicious activity. When the robot was named John and had a male voice, it was rated as more useful than when it was named Joan and had a female voice—even though John and Joan did identical work. Other research has documented the opposite effect for robots that operate within the home.

Finally, humanoid robots can create interpersonal issues in the workplace. In the Snackbot experiment, one person felt awkward when the robot commented, within earshot of other employees, on how much that participant liked to order Reese's Peanut Butter Cups. Another expressed jealousy after Snackbot complimented a colleague for being in the office all the time and therefore being a hard worker. "The more you add lifelike characteristics, and particularly the more you add things that seem like emotion, the more strongly it evokes these social effects," says Jonathan Gratch, a professor at the University of Southern California who studies human-machine interactions. "It's not always clear that you want your virtual robot teammate to be just like a person. You want it to be *better* than a person."

In his own research Gratch has explored how thinking machines might get the best of both worlds, eliciting humans' trust while avoiding some of the pitfalls of anthropomorphism. In one study he had participants in two groups discuss their health with a digitally animated figure on a television screen (dubbed a "virtual human"). One group was told that people were controlling the avatar; the other group was told that the avatar was fully automated. Those in the latter group were willing to disclose more about their health and even displayed more sadness. "When they're being talked to by a person, they fear being negatively judged," Gratch says.

Gratch hypothesizes that "in certain circumstances the lack of humanness of the machine is better." For instance, "you might imagine that if you had a computer boss, you would be more likely to be truthful about what its shortcomings were." And in some cases, Gratch thinks, less humanoid robots would even be perceived as less susceptible to bias or favoritism.

When People Prefer Robot Colleagues

How we work with thinking machines will vary according to the work we're doing, how it's framed, and how the machines are designed. But under the right conditions, people are surprisingly open to a robotic coworker. Julie Shah and her colleagues at MIT set up an experiment in which a participant, an assistant, and a robot collaborated to build Lego kits. They were told to approach the job as if they were working in manufacturing and had a tight deadline to complete the work. Allocating tasks effectively among team members was critical to completing the project quickly.

Participants built three kits under three different conditions. In one case, the robot assigned the tasks—fetching Lego parts from one bench, assembling them on another. In the second case, the participant assigned the tasks. In the third case, the participant scheduled his or her own work, while the robot allocated the remaining tasks to itself and the assistant. The researchers guessed that the participants would be most satisfied in the third scenario, because they would get some benefit from the robot's algorithmic expertise in scheduling but would also have autonomy over their own work. In fact people preferred having the robot assign all the tasks. That was also the most efficient scenario: Teams took the least time to complete the project.

Why were these participants so much more accepting than the ones at Wharton who refused to rely on an algorithm? We don't yet know enough to say for sure. Shah points to the fact that the task was difficult to complete in the required time frame, so people recognized that they would benefit from the robot's help. How the work was framed most likely helped too: The goal was to maximize productivity in a controlled environment while racing against the clock—the sort of logical challenge a robot might be good at meeting. Finally, although the robot had no voice and wasn't designed to be social, it did have a body, which may have made it seem more intelligent than a disembodied algorithm.

At the end of Shah's experiment the participants gave feedback about why they preferred one scenario over the others. Tellingly, those who preferred having the robot in charge didn't emphasize its humanoid qualities or the bonds they had formed with it. Instead they gave reasons such as "I never felt like I was wasting time" and "It removes the possibility of scheduling being influenced by the ego of the team leader." The robot made a great teammate because it did what robots do best.

Originally published in June 2015. Reprint R1506F

Managing Our Hub Economy

by Marco Iansiti and Karim R. Lakhani

THE GLOBAL ECONOMY IS COALESCING around a few digital super-powers. We see unmistakable evidence that a winner-take-all world is emerging in which a small number of "hub firms"— including Alibaba, Alphabet/Google, Amazon, Apple, Baidu, Facebook, Microsoft, and Tencent—occupy central positions. While creating real value for users, these companies are also capturing a disproportionate and expanding share of the value, and that's shaping our collective economic future. The very same technologies that promised to democratize business are now threatening to make it more monopolistic.

Beyond dominating individual markets, hub firms create and control essential connections in the networks that pervade our economy. Google's Android and related technologies form "competitive bottlenecks"; that is, they own access to billions of mobile consumers that other product and service providers want to reach. Google can not only exact a toll on transactions but also influence the flow of information and the data collected. Amazon's and Alibaba's marketplaces also connect vast numbers of users with large numbers of retailers and manufacturers. Tencent's WeChat messaging platform aggregates a billion global users and provides a critical source of consumer access for businesses offering online banking, entertainment, transportation, and other services. The more users who join these networks, the more attractive (and even necessary) it becomes for enterprises to offer their products and services through them. By driving increasing returns to scale and controlling crucial competitive bottlenecks, these digital superpowers can become even mightier, extract disproportionate value, and tip the global competitive balance.

Hub firms don't compete in a traditional fashion—vying with existing products or services, perhaps with improved features or lower cost. Rather, they take the network-based assets that have already reached scale in one setting and then use them to enter another industry and "re-architect" its competitive structure— transforming it from product-driven to network-driven. They plug adjacent industries into the same competitive bottlenecks they already control.

For example, the Alibaba spin-off Ant Financial does not simply offer better payment services, a better credit card, or an improved investment management service; it builds on data from Alibaba's already vast user base to commoditize traditional financial services and reorganize a good chunk of the Chinese financial sector around the Ant Financial platform. The three-year-old service already has over half a billion users and plans to expand well beyond China. Similarly, Google's automotive strategy does not simply entail creating an improved car; it leverages technologies and data advantages (many already at scale from billions of mobile consumers and millions of advertisers) to change the structure of the auto industry itself. (Disclosure: Both of us work or have worked with some of the firms mentioned in this article.)

If current trends continue, the hub economy will spread across more industries, further concentrating data, value, and power in the hands of a small number of firms employing a tiny fraction of the workforce. Disparity in firm valuation and individual wealth already causes widespread resentment. Over time, we can expect consumers, regulators, and even social movements to take an increasingly hostile stand against this concentration of value and economic connectivity. In a painfully ironic turn, after creating unprecedented opportunity across the global economy, digitization—and the trends it has given rise to—could exacerbate already dangerous levels of income inequality, undermine the economy, and even lead to social instability.

Idea in Brief

The Situation

A few digital superpowers, or hub firms, are capturing a disproportionate and growing share of the value being created in the global economy.

The Challenge

This trend threatens to exacerbate already dangerous levels of income inequality, undermine the economy, and destabilize society.

The Answer

While there are ways for companies that depend on hubs to defend their positions, the hubs themselves will have to do more to share economic value and sustain stakeholders.

Can these trends be reversed? We believe not. The "hub economy," as we will argue, is here to stay. But most companies will not become hubs, and they will need to respond astutely to the growing concentration of hub power. Digitizing operating capabilities will not be enough. Digital messaging platforms, for example, have already dealt a blow to telecom service providers; investment advisors still face threats from online financial-services companies. To remain competitive, companies will need to use their assets and capabilities differently, transform their core businesses, develop new revenue opportunities, and identify areas that can be defended from encroaching hub firms and others rushing in from previously disconnected economic sectors. Some companies have started on this path—Comcast, with its new Xfinity platform, is a notable example—but the majority, especially those in traditional sectors, still need to master the implications of network competition.

Most importantly, the very same hub firms that are transforming our economy must be part of the solution—and their leaders must step up. As Mark Zuckerberg articulated in his Harvard commencement address in May 2017, "we have a level of wealth inequality that hurts everyone." Business as usual is not a good option. Witness the public concern about the roles that Facebook and Twitter played in the recent U.S. presidential election, Google's challenges with global regulatory bodies, criticism of Uber's culture and operating policies, and complaints that Airbnb's rental practices are racially discriminatory and harmful to municipal housing stocks, rents, and pricing.

Thoughtful hub strategies will create effective ways to share economic value, manage collective risks, and sustain the networks and communities we all ultimately depend on. If carmakers, major retailers, or media companies continue to go out of business, massive economic and social dislocation will ensue. And with governments and public opinion increasingly attuned to this problem, hub strategies that foster a more stable economy and united society will drive differentiation among the hub firms themselves.

We are encouraged by Facebook's response to the public outcry over "fake news"—hiring thousands of dedicated employees, shutting down tens of thousands of phony accounts, working with news sources to identify untrue claims, and offering guides for spotting false information. Similarly, Google's YouTube division invests in engineering, artificial intelligence, and human resources and collaborates with NGOs to ensure that videos promoting political extremists and terrorists are taken down promptly.

A real opportunity exists for hub firms to truly lead our economy. This will require hubs to fully consider the long-term societal impact of their decisions and to prioritize their ethical responsibilities to the large economic ecosystems that increasingly revolve around them. At the same time, the rest of us—whether in established enterprises or start-ups, in institutions or communities—will need to serve as checks and balances, helping to shape the hub economy by providing critical, informed input and, as needed, pushback.

The Digital Domino Effect

The emergence of economic hubs is rooted in three principles of digitization and network theory. The first is Moore's law, which states that computer processing power will double approximately every two years. The implication is that performance improvements will continue driving the augmentation and replacement of human activity with digital tools. This affects any industry that has integrated computers into its operations—which pretty much covers the entire economy. And advances in machine learning and cloud computing have only reinforced this trend.

The second principle involves connectivity. Most computing devices today have built-in network connectivity that allows them to communicate with one another. Modern digital technology enables the sharing of information at near-zero marginal cost, and digital networks are spreading rapidly. Metcalfe's law states that a network's value increases with the number of nodes (connection points) or users—the dynamic we think of as network effects. This means that digital technology is enabling significant growth in value across our economy, particularly as open-network connections allow for the recombination of business offerings, such as the migration from payment tools to the broader financial services and insurance that we've seen at Ant Financial.

But while value is being created for everyone, value capture is getting more skewed and concentrated. This is because in networks, traffic begets more traffic, and as certain nodes become more heavily used, they attract additional attachments, which further increases their importance. This brings us to the third principle, a lesser-known dynamic originally posited by the physicist Albert-László Barabási: the notion that digital-network formation naturally leads to the emergence of positive feedback loops that create increasingly important, highly connected hubs. As digital networks carry more and more economic transactions, the economic power of network hubs, which connect consumers, firms, and even industries to one another, expands. Once a hub is highly connected (and enjoying increasing returns to scale) in one sector of the economy (such as mobile telecommunications), it will enjoy a crucial advantage as it begins to connect in a new sector (automobiles, for example). This can, in turn, drive more and more markets to tip, and the many players competing in traditionally separate industries get winnowed down to just a few hub firms that capture a growing share of the overall economic value created—a kind of digital domino effect.

This phenomenon isn't new. But in recent years, the high degree of digital connectivity has dramatically sped up the transformation. Just a few years ago, cell phone manufacturers competed head-to-head for industry leadership in a traditional product market without appreciable network effects. Competition led to innovation and differentiation, with a business model delivering healthy profitability at scale for a dozen or so major competitors. But with the introduction of iOS and Android, the industry began to tip away from its hardware centricity to network structures centered on these multisided platforms. The platforms connected smartphones to a large number of apps and services. Each new app makes the platform it sits on more valuable, creating a powerful network effect that in turn creates a more daunting barrier to entry for new players. Today Motorola, Nokia, BlackBerry, and Palm are out of the mobile phone business, and Google and Apple are extracting the lion's share of the sector's value. The value captured by the large majority of complementors—the app developers and third-party manufacturers—is generally modest at best.

The domino effect is now spreading to other sectors and picking up speed. Music has already tipped to Apple, Google, and Spotify. E-commerce is following a similar path: Alibaba and Amazon are gaining more share and moving into traditional brick-and-mortar strongholds like groceries (witness Amazon's acquisition of Whole Foods). We've already noted the growing power of WeChat in messaging and communications; along with Facebook and others, it's challenging traditional telecom service providers. On-premise computer and software offerings are losing ground to the cloud services provided by Amazon, Microsoft, Google, and Alibaba. In financial services, the big players are Ant, Paytm, Ingenico, and the independent start-up Wealthfront; in home entertainment, Amazon, Apple, Google, and Netflix dominate.

Where are powerful hub firms likely to emerge next? Health care, industrial products, and agriculture are three contenders. But let's examine how the digital domino effect could play out in another prime candidate, the automotive sector, which in the United States alone provides more than seven million jobs and generates close to a trillion dollars in yearly sales.

Re-architecting the Automotive Sector

As with many other products and services, cars are now connected to digital networks, essentially becoming rolling information and transaction nodes. This connectivity is reshaping the structure of the automotive industry. When cars were merely products, car sales were the main prize. But a new source of value is emerging: the connection to consumers in transit. Americans spend almost an hour, on average, getting to and from work every day, and commutes keep getting longer. Auto manufacturers, responding to consumer demand, have already given hub firms access to dashboard screens in many cars; drivers can use Apple or Google apps on the car's built-in display instead of on their smartphones. If consumers embrace self-driving vehicles, that one hour of consumer access could be worth hundreds of billions of dollars in the U.S. alone.

Which companies will capitalize on the vast commercial potential of a new hour of free time for the world's car commuters? Hub firms like Alphabet and Apple are first in line. They already have bottleneck assets like maps and advertising networks at scale, and both are ready to create super-relevant ads pinpointed to the car's passengers and location. One logical add-on feature for autonomous vehicles would be a "Drive there" button that appears when an ad pops up (as already happens on Google's Waze app); pressing it would order the car to head to the touted destination.

In a future when people are no longer behind the wheel, cars will become less about the driving experience and more about the apps and services offered by automobiles as they ferry passengers around. Apart from a minority of cars actually driven for fun, differentiation will lessen, and the vehicle itself might well become commoditized. That will threaten manufacturers' core business: The car features that buyers will care most about—software and networks—will be largely outside the automakers' control, and their price premiums will go down.

The transformation will also upend a range of connected sectors—including insurance, automotive repairs and maintenance, road construction, law enforcement, and infrastructure—as the digital dominos continue to fall. (See the exhibit "The connected-car ecosystem.")

The connected-car ecosystem

Three software platforms—Android Auto, Apple CarPlay, and, to a lesser extent, OpenCar—dominate the market for integrating smartphone functionality into vehicles. They constitute powerful bottleneck assets because they have scores of supply-chain partners (left) and they enable other stakeholders (right) to reach consumers. (Note: The companies, apps, and regulators listed are selected examples only.)

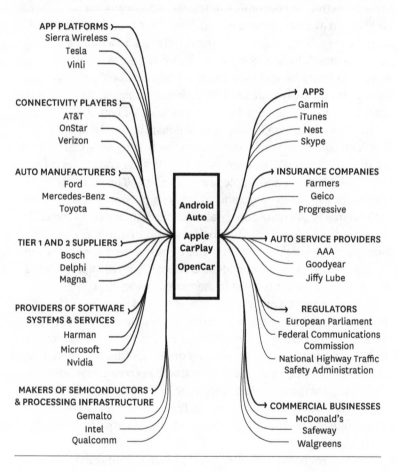

APP PLATFORMS
Sierra Wireless
Tesla
Vinli

CONNECTIVITY PLAYERS
AT&T
OnStar
Verizon

AUTO MANUFACTURERS
Ford
Mercedes-Benz
Toyota

TIER 1 AND 2 SUPPLIERS
Bosch
Delphi
Magna

PROVIDERS OF SOFTWARE
SYSTEMS & SERVICES
Harman
Microsoft
Nvidia

MAKERS OF SEMICONDUCTORS
& PROCESSING INFRASTRUCTURE
Gemalto
Intel
Qualcomm

Android Auto
Apple CarPlay
OpenCar

APPS
Garmin
iTunes
Nest
Skype

INSURANCE COMPANIES
Farmers
Geico
Progressive

AUTO SERVICE PROVIDERS
AAA
Goodyear
Jiffy Lube

REGULATORS
European Parliament
Federal Communications Commission
National Highway Traffic Safety Administration

COMMERCIAL BUSINESSES
McDonald's
Safeway
Walgreens

For existing auto manufacturers, the picture is grim but not hopeless. Some companies are exploring a pay-per-use model for their cars and are acquiring, launching, or partnering with car-as-a-service providers. GM, for one, invested $500 million in the ride-sharing service Lyft, and its luxury-car division is now offering a monthly car subscription service. Daimler launched a car-sharing business called car2go. Several manufacturers have also invested in their own research into driverless vehicles or part-nered with external providers.

Beyond these business-model experiments, automakers will need to play as the hubs do, by participating in the platform competition that will determine value capture in the sector. At least for the moment, alternatives to Google and Apple are scarce. One example is OpenCar, recently acquired by Inrix, a traditional auto supplier. Unlike Apple CarPlay and Google's Android Auto, which limit automaker-specific customization and require access to proprietary car data, the OpenCar framework is fully controlled by the car manufacturer. To take on the established giants, we believe that OpenCar and Inrix will have to develop an effective advertising or commerce platform or adopt some other indirect monetization strategy—and to do that, they'll probably need to partner with companies that have those capabilities.

To reach the scale required to be competitive, automotive com-panies that were once fierce rivals may need to join together. Here Technologies, which provides precision mapping data and location services, is an interesting example. Here has its roots in Navteq, one of the early online mapping companies, which was first bought by Nokia and later acquired by a consortium of Volkswagen, BMW, and Daimler (the multibillion-dollar price tag may have been too high for any single carmaker to stomach). Here provides third-party devel-opers with sophisticated tools and APIs for creating location-based ads and other services. The company represents an attempt by auto manufacturers to assemble a "federated" platform and, in doing so, neutralize the threat of a potential competitive bottleneck controlled by Google and Apple. The consortium could play a significant role in preventing automotive value capture from tipping completely toward existing hub firms.

Of course, successful collaboration depends on a common, strongly felt commitment. So as traditional enterprises position themselves for a fight, they must understand how the competitive dynamics in their industries have shifted.

Increasing Returns to Scale Are Hard to Beat

Competitive advantage in many industries is moderated by *decreasing* returns to scale. In traditional product and service businesses, the value creation curve typically flattens out as the number of consumers increases, as we see in the exhibit "Profiting from a growing customer base." A firm gains no particular advantage as its user base continues to increase beyond already efficient levels, which enables multiple competitors to coexist.

Profiting from a growing customer base

For traditional product and service businesses, gaining additional customers does not continue adding commensurate value after a certain point. However, many platform businesses (Amazon, Facebook, and the like) become more and more valuable as more people and companies use them, connect with one another, and create network effects.

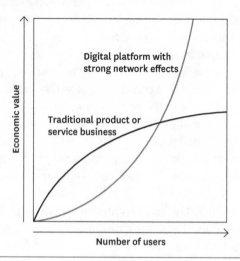

Some digital technologies, however, exhibit *increasing* returns to scale. A local advertising platform gets better and better as more and more users attract more and more ads. And as the number of ads increases, so does the ability to target the ads to the users, making individual ads more valuable. An advertising platform is thus similar to software platforms such as Windows, Linux, Android, and iOS, which exhibit increasing returns to scale—their growing value to consumers increases the number of available apps, while the value to app developers rises as the number of consumers rises. The more consumers, the greater the incentive for developers to build apps, and the more apps there are, the more motivated consumers are to use their digital devices.

These considerations are important to the nature of hub competition. The economics of traditional decreasing returns make it possible for several competitors to coexist and provide differentiated value to attract users. That's the dynamic in the auto industry today, with many car manufacturers competing with one another to offer a variety of differentiated products. But the increasing returns in digital assets like ad platforms (or possibly driverless-car technology) will heighten the advantage of the competitor with the largest scale, the largest network of users, or the most data. And this is where the hub firms will most likely leverage their large and growing lead—and cause value to concentrate around them.

In contrast with traditional product and service businesses, network-based markets exhibiting increasing returns to scale will, over time, tip toward a narrow set of players. This implies that if a conventional decreasing-returns business (say, telecom or media) is threatened by a new type of competitor whose business model experiences increasing returns, the conventional player is in for a rough ride. With increasing returns to scale, a digital technology can provide a bottleneck to an entire industrial sector. And left alone, competitive bottlenecks dramatically skew value capture away from traditional firms.

Pushing Back

Hub firms often compete against one another. Microsoft has made substantial investments in augmented reality in an effort to create a new hub and counterbalance the power that Google and Apple wield in the mobile space. Facebook acquired Oculus to force a similar structural shift in the emerging field of virtual reality. And a battle is looming in the smart-home arena, as Google, Apple, Microsoft, and Samsung attempt to reduce Amazon's early lead in voice-activated home technology.

But how does the rest of the economy deal with the increasing returns to scale of hub firms? With enough foresight and investment, traditional firms can resist by becoming hubs themselves, as we are seeing especially in the internet of things (IoT) space. GE is the classic example of this approach, with its investment in the Predix platform and the creation of GE Digital. Other companies are following suit in different settings—for example, Verizon and Vodafone with their IoT platforms.

Firms can also shape competition by investing to ensure that there are multiple hubs in each sector—and even influencing which ones win. They can organize to support less-established platforms, thus making a particular hub more viable and an industry sector more competitive in the long term. Deutsche Telekom, for instance, is partnering with Microsoft Azure (rather than Amazon Web Services) for cloud computing in Central Europe.

Most importantly, the value generated by networks will change as firms compete, innovate, and respond to community and regulatory pressure. Multihoming—a practice enabling participants on one hub's ecosystem to easily join another—can significantly mitigate the rise of hub power. For example, drivers and passengers routinely multihome across different ride-sharing platforms, often checking prices on Uber, Lyft, and Fasten to see which is offering the best deal. Retailers are starting to multihome across payment systems, supporting multiple solutions (such as Apple Pay, Google Wallet, and Samsung Pay). If multihoming is common, the market is less likely to tip to a single player, preserving competition and diffusing value capture. Indeed, companies will need to make their products and services available on multiple hubs and encourage the formation of new hubs to avoid being held hostage by one dominant player. Take the wireless-speaker manufacturer Sonos: It has ensured that its music system seamlessly integrates with as many music services as possible, including Apple Music, Amazon Music Unlimited, Google Play Music, Pandora, Spotify, and Tidal.

Collective action can also restructure economic networks, shape value creation and capture, and ease competitive bottlenecks. In the 1990s the open-source community organized to compete against Microsoft Windows with the Linux operating system. That effort was actively supported by traditional players such as IBM and Hewlett-Packard and reinforced later by Google and Facebook. Today Linux (and Linux-related products) are firmly established in enterprises, consumer devices, and cloud computing. Similarly, the Mozilla open-source community and its Firefox browser broke Microsoft's grip on navigating the internet. Even Apple, notorious for its proprietary approach, relies on open-source software for its core operating systems and web services, and the infamous iPhone jailbreaking craze demonstrated both the extraordinary demand for third-party apps and the burgeoning supply of them.

Open source has grown beyond all expectations to create an increasingly essential legacy of common intellectual property, capabilities, and methodologies. Now collective action is going well beyond code sharing to include coordination on data aggregation, the use of common infrastructure, and the standardization of practices to further equilibrate the power of hubs. Efforts like OpenStreetMap are leading the way in maps, and Mozilla's Common Voice project is crowdsourcing global voice data to open up the speech-recognition bottleneck.

Collective action will be increasingly crucial to sustaining balance in the digital economy. As economic sectors coalesce into networks and as powerful hubs continue to form, other stakeholders will need to work together to ensure that hubs look after the interests of all network members. Cooperation will become more important for the rivals that orbit hubs; indeed, strategic joint action by companies that are not hubs may be the best competitive antidote to the rising power of hub firms.

The public is also raising concerns about privacy, online tracking, cybersecurity, and data aggregation. Solutions being suggested include requirements for social network and data portability similar to the requirements for phone number portability that telecommunications regulators instituted to increase competition among phone service providers.

The Ethics of Network Leadership

The responsibility for sustaining our (digital) economy rests partly with the same leaders who are poised to control it. By developing such central positions of power and influence, hub firms have become de facto stewards of the long-term health of our economy. Leaders of hub companies need to realize that their organizations are analogous to "keystone" species in biological ecosystems—playing a critical role in maintaining their surroundings. Apple, Alibaba, Alphabet/Google, Amazon, and others that benefit disproportionately from the ecosystems they dominate have rational and ethical reasons to support the economic vitality of not just their direct participants but also the broader industries they serve. In particular, we argue that hub companies need to incorporate value *sharing* into their business models, along with value creation and value capture.

Building and maintaining a healthy ecosystem is in the best interests of hub companies. Amazon and Alibaba claim millions of marketplace sellers, and they profit from every transaction those merchants make. Similarly, Google and Apple earn billions in revenue from the third-party apps that run on their platforms. Both companies already invest heavily in the developer community, providing programming frameworks, software tools, and opportunities and business models that enable developers to grow their businesses. But such efforts will need to be scaled up and refined as hub firms find themselves at the center of—and relying on—much larger and more-complex ecosystems. Preserving the strength and productivity of complementary communities should be a fundamental part of any hub firm's strategy.

Uber provides an interesting example of the repercussions of getting this wrong. Uber's viability depends on its relations with its drivers and riders, who have often criticized the company's practices. Under pressure from those communities—and from competitors that offer drivers the potential to earn more—Uber is making improvements. Still, its challenges suggest that no hub will maintain an advantage over the long term if it neglects the well-being of its ecosystem partners. Microsoft learned a hard lesson when it failed to maintain the health of its PC software ecosystem, losing out to the Linux community in cloud services.

But network ethics are not just about financial considerations; social concerns are equally important. Centralized platforms, such as Kiva for charitable impact investing and Airbnb for accommodation bookings, have been found to be susceptible to racial discrimination. In Airbnb's case, external researchers convincingly demonstrated that African-American guests were especially likely to have their reservation requests rejected. The pressure is now on Airbnb to fight bias both by educating its proprietors and by modifying certain platform features. Additionally, as Airbnb continues to grow, it must work to ensure that its hosts heed municipal regulations, lest they face a potentially devastating regulatory backlash.

Indeed, if hubs do not promote the health and sustainability of the many firms and individuals in their networks, other forces will undoubtedly step in. Governments and regulators will increasingly act to encourage competition, protect consumer welfare, and foster economic stability. Consider the challenges Google faces in Europe, where regulators are concerned about the dominance of both its search advertising business and its Android platform.

The centralizing forces of digitization are not going to slow down anytime soon. The emergence of powerful hub firms is well under way, and the threats to global economic well-being are unmistakable. All actors in the economy—but particularly the hub firms themselves—should work to sustain the entire ecosystem and observe new principles, for both strategic and ethical reasons. Otherwise, we are all in serious trouble.

Originally published in September–October 2017. Reprint R1705F

CHRIS ANDERSON is the CEO of 3DR. He was formerly Editor-in-Chief of *Wired* and is author of *The Long Tail: Why the Future of Business Is Selling Less of More.*

PAUL R. DAUGHERTY is a managing director of information technology and business research at Accenture Research. He is a coauthor (with H. James Wilson) of *Human + Machine: Reimagining Work in the Age of AI* (Harvard Business Review Press, 2018).

RICHARD A. D'AVENI is the Bakala Professor of Strategy at Dartmouth's Tuck School of Business. He is the author of several HBR articles and the book *The Pan-Industrial Revolution: How New Manufacturing Titans Will Transform the World.*

THOMAS H. DAVENPORT is the President's Distinguished Professor of Information Technology and Management at Babson College, a research fellow at the MIT Initiative on the Digital Economy, and a senior adviser at Deloitte Analytics.

NIRAJ DAWAR is a professor of marketing at the Ivey Business School and the author of *Tilt: Shifting Your Strategy from Products to Customers* (Harvard Business Review Press, 2013).

WALTER FRICK is a senior editor at *Harvard Business Review.*

JAMES E. HEPPELMANN is the president and CEO of PTC, a leading maker of industrial software.

MARCO IANSITI is the David Sarnoff Professor of Business Administration at Harvard Business School, where he heads the Technology and Operations Management Unit and the Digital Initiative.

JON KLEINBERG is a professor of computer science at Cornell University and the coauthor of the textbooks *Algorithm Design* (with Éva Tardos) and *Networks, Crowds, and Markets* (with David Easley).

KATRINA LAKE is the CEO of Stitch Fix.

KARIM R. LAKHANI is a professor of business administration at Harvard Business School and the founding director of the Harvard Innovation Science Laboratory.

MICHAEL LUCA is the Lee J. Styslinger III Associate Professor of Business Administration at Harvard Business School.

SENDHIL MULLAINATHAN is a professor of economics at Harvard University and the coauthor (with Eldar Shafir) of *Scarcity: Why Having Too Little Means So Much.*

MICHAEL E. PORTER is a University Professor at Harvard, based at Harvard Business School.

RAJEEV RONANKI is a principal at Deloitte Consulting, where he leads the cognitive computing and health care innovation practices. Some of the companies mentioned in his article are Deloitte clients.

H. JAMES WILSON is a managing director of information technology and business research at Accenture Research. He is a coauthor (with Paul Daugherty) of *Human + Machine: Reimagining Work in the Age of AI* (Harvard Business Review Press, 2018).

Index

The most important management ideas all in one place.

We hope you enjoyed this book from *Harvard Business Review*. Now you can get even more with HBR's 10 Must Reads Boxed Set. From books on leadership and strategy to managing yourself and others, this 6-book collection delivers articles on the most essential business topics to help you succeed.

HBR's 10 Must Reads Series

The definitive collection of ideas and best practices on our most sought-after topics from the best minds in business.

- Change Management
- Collaboration
- Communication
- Emotional Intelligence
- Innovation
- Leadership
- Making Smart Decisions

- Managing Across Cultures
- Managing People
- Managing Yourself
- Strategic Marketing
- Strategy
- Teams
- The Essentials

hbr.org/mustreads

CPSIA information can be obtained
at www.ICGtesting.com
Printed in the USA
BVHW031226180821
614692BV00001B/34